THE GOOD NEWS

ACCORDING to MATTHEW

THE GOOD NEWS

ACCORDING to MATTHEW

A TRAINING MANUAL
FOR PROPHETS

PAUL S. MINEAR

Chalice Press®

St. Louis, Missouri

Cover art: © Comstock, Inc., 1998
Cover and interior design: Elizabeth Wright
Art direction: Elizabeth Wright

This book is printed on acid-free, recycled paper.

Visit Chalice Press on the World Wide Web at
www.chalicepress.com

10   9   8   7   6   5   4   3   2   1   00   01   02   03   04   05

Library of Congress Cataloging–in–Publication Data

Minear, Paul Sevier, 1906–
    The Good News according to Matthew : a training manual for prophets / Paul S. Minear.
        p.   cm.
    Includes bibliographical references and index.
    ISBN 0-8272-1245-3
    1. Bible. N. T. Matthew–Criticism, interpretation, etc.   I. Title.
    BS2575.2   .M55   2000
    226.2'06–dc21
                                                                    00-009091

Printed in the United States of America

To
Gladys
for immense help
in all my writing
(1936–1997)

CONTENTS

PREFACE

I recall many efforts in years past to introduce students to the gospel of Matthew. In a course dubbed "New Testament Introduction" we usually began with what were considered the most essential questions: Who was the author? When and where was he writing? For what audience? What were the sources of his information about Jesus? How did his picture of Jesus compare with other ancient pictures? I must now confess to a haunting frustration with such an approach. To be sure, we collected a certain amount of data for notebooks and minds, but that data helped little in bridging the intangible distances between Matthew's mind and our own. Often the data treated as primary many matters with which Matthew was not concerned. At best, our methods succeeded only in forcing Matthew into the world where we felt most at home, a world with our latitudes and longitudes, our time charts, and our historical objectivities. Because our own world remained fixed, reactions to his thought remained subject to our own prejudgments–very modern students being trained to be quite sophisticated in dealing with a remote artifact.

If I were to teach that course again, I would concentrate on finding ways to penetrate Matthew's thought-world, that universe within which he felt most at home. The only way to do that is to take seriously the integrity of his language-world. It is only there that we can have a heart-to-heart talk with him. His world was dominated by devotion to Jesus as a slave-Messiah; it had been shaken to its core by the story of Jesus' shame and glory. On his side of that earthquake, the world was divided between believers, who daily risked their lives for this heavenly Lord, and adversaries, who considered it their holy duty to vilify such believers. Whatever his name may have been, this author belonged to that world of heartfelt loyalty and violence. We cannot enter into his world until we recover a lively sense of the grounds for such loyalty–and such violence.

There is much about him, of course, that would be of substantial help if we could only recover it: his name and residence, his personal biography before and after he began to follow the Messiah, the precise cluster of obligations that he had accepted in becoming a leader in this maverick community. On such matters we must sift the evidence, however scattered and uncertain, and form tentative conclusions. But there are more important matters that a careful reading of the Gospel may reveal, where inferences may be drawn with greater confidence.

Matthew was concerned in a major way, for example, with the education of Simon Peter. Because this disciple was typical of the other disciples, and on many occasions was their spokesman, Jesus' concern for his training serves as a case study of his efforts to prepare all his apostles-designate to carry on his work after his death. It is obvious that the story of Jesus remained central, but it is equally certain that Jesus viewed the training of these future fishermen as central to his own assignment. They, of course, depended on him; but he also depended on them. And what was true for Jesus was as true for Matthew. In almost every chapter he was concerned to show Jesus' failures and successes in educating those carefully selected successors. This concern on Matthew's part entitles us to imagine that he, too, felt committed to carrying on the vocation of those whom Jesus sent into the harvest fields.

Believing this to be true of the "biographer" of Jesus and of Peter, I think that Matthew has a special relevance for students of theology. Their calling into the Christian ministry gives them a special bond to the narrator of this Gospel; they have a shared interest in recovering a clear view of how Jesus trained the twelve disciples to meet the needs of the wider circle of followers. Not only should this bond help them to spot certain similarities between Peter's training and their own, but it should also alert their imaginations to discern why Matthew reported Jesus' actions and words as he did. By viewing this Gospel as the first authoritative training manual, originally designed for the apostles and their first replacements, students may find that in a mysterious way this Gospel becomes their own study syllabus as they prepare for pursuing their own calling by the same teacher.

I present this essay as a result of a recent rereading of the Gospel. What follows is not old stuff to me but my reactions to a fresh encounter with the mind of the author during the past three years. In this encounter I have not relied on the vast library of scholarly research, though I do not discount the value of earlier studies. Rather, by concentrating on the entirety of the Gospel itself, as a literary work designed by an individual writer for a very specific audience, I have tried to recover his world of thought and devotion. I do not know whether this focus commends itself to my readers, but I wish that I had pursued such a project of study at the outset of my theological training.

Four friends have read the entire manuscript, Brevard Childs, J. Louis Martyn, Robert Raines, and Gaylord Noyce–and I have profited from their comments. I am grateful to them and also to Robert and Brenda Whitaker for secretarial expertise.

At the beginning of their study of this Gospel, all readers can profit from the advice of John Bunyan in his preface to *The Pilgrim's Progress:*

> The prophets used much by metaphors
> To set forth truth; yea who considers
> Christ, his apostles too, shall plainly see
> That truths to this day in such mantles be.

CHAPTER 1

IMAGINING THE REAL

My thoughts are not your thoughts,
nor are your ways my ways, says the LORD.

(Isaiah 55:8)

The Lord who said this through Isaiah is the God of the entire Bible. This terse axiom contains and conceals many vital accents in biblical thinking. This God is a Lord who speaks; this God is no silent or passive spectator of the human scene, but a God concerned with the thoughts and the ways of God's people. God can use many voices; in this case God uses the voice of the prophet. But when God speaks, mortals become aware of a perilous distance between their understanding of God and God's will for them. Of that peril Isaiah was more acutely aware than were his people. He was no simpleton, no undisciplined thinker; yet he was baffled by God's distance, and more baffled than were his readers. Isaiah was sure of one thing: The Lord's thoughts and ways form an ultimate horizon beyond which mortals can perceive no other.[1] God's *thoughts* extend far beyond the reach of human wisdom; God's *ways* constitute a real world that can only be imagined. Human imagination is perverted when it serves as a projection of human desires and devices; it can be trusted only when God takes the initiative in disclosing God's thoughts and ways to that imagination. To imagine the real is to

1

perceive the hidden origins and outcomes of human thoughts and ways, for such origins are known only to God, and God alone controls those outcomes. These are some of the implications to be inferred from Isaiah's axiom.

In this study of Matthew, we begin, then, by recognizing the biblical insight that the real can only be imagined.[2] This imagination, in turn, must recognize that the entire Gospel comes to us in the form of a story, a single story in which every episode is linked to every other episode. In this all-inclusive story, the narrator embodied a triple perspective. In telling each episode or teaching, he was concerned to realize three distinct objectives, each of which reflected motives that were at once personal and literary.

Three Perspectives

The first perspective was one in which the narrator invited readers to imagine the story of Jesus from his birth to his death, moving steadily from one body of teachings to an ensuing cluster of episodes, and then from another body of teachings (there were five "sermons" in all) to other episodes, with their anticipated conflicts and consequences. In this way, the scribe reported what he considered to be most important in the traditions he inherited, from Jesus' baptism by John to his final command to his disciples to baptize other disciples in his name. He recounted each successive teaching and episode in such a way as to add to the readers' comprehension of how Jesus had completed his messianic assignment to the villages of Israel. The care with which the editor linked these traditions together indicates the importance he attached to this perspective: looking forward with Jesus and his disciples from the beginning to the consummation of his assignment from God. The continued story of Jesus' vocation was carefully constructed to disclose the hidden thoughts and ways of God. We may call this the "vocation of Jesus" perspective.[3]

A second perspective both embodied and reflected the emerging vocation of the disciples, among whom I think Matthew included himself. Within the church of his day he was clearly one of the leaders whose calling combined a complex pattern of duties and goals. In literary terms, his was the work of a scribe who "brings out of his treasure what is new and what is old" (13:52). He was also a teacher who recognized an obligation to relay from the Master-teacher commands that were designed for "the little ones" in his own church. At the same time, his sensibilities were those of a prophet who discerned in the work of Jesus hidden things that "prophets and kings had long hoped to see and to hear" (13:17, au. trans.). His work as teacher, scribe, and prophet made him a mediator between the first band of apostolic messengers and his own newly born community. It is, of course, possible that he was himself one of the Twelve or one of those who became followers even before Golgotha. More probably, he had responded to the message of the kingdom as he had heard it from one of the initial apostles from whom he had also received a share in proclaiming the good news, in casting out demons, and in training other believers in the basics of their vocation. We should probably assume that he thought of himself as one of the "prophets, sages, and scribes" whom Jesus promised to send to a Jerusalem that would reject them for the same reasons it had rejected him (23:34ff.). Writing from such a vantage point, this teacher-scribe-prophet looked back with his readers over the entire course of Jesus' vocation, a vocation willed by God.

Such a vocationally charged retrospective casts fresh light on those earliest years. Interest was now focused to a special degree on Jesus' concern for the legacy that he would leave for his apostles. Two features of that legacy should be cited, because they determined the conditions of this postresurrection assignment. The first was the recurrent demand that all who followed Jesus must bear his cross and thus share in the new covenant in his blood. In his first sermon on a mountain, Jesus announced in God's name a blessing on those who would be persecuted like "the prophets who were before you" (5:12). The graphic details of such persecution were spelled out in his instructions for their first field-work project (10:16–33). The same prospect was outlined as he prepared to enter rebellious Jerusalem for the last time (23:34ff.); it became a part of his final mountain sermon (24:9–14).

A second feature of Jesus' legacy was the clear and consistent identification of future adversaries.[4] His followers would be dragged before "governors and kings," to be sure, but it was religious leaders who would initiate such legal action. The current Jerusalem was "the city that kills the prophets" (23:37). When Jesus sent out his sheep among the wolves, those wolves would attack them primarily in synagogues and before councils (10:16–22). An even greater danger to the movement, however, would arise within the church itself, from false prophets who would deceive and mislead the elect (7:15, 22, 26; 10:37–42; 16:23; 18:6–14; 22:11–14; 24:11, 24, 45–51; 25:41–46). Such was the vocational retrospect and prospect of the

Evangelist, who desired above all else to be a true prophet, a faithful scribe, and a courageous witness-martyr.

The third perspective was provided by the creative design of God, which for Matthew provided the baseline from which to think about the entire story of Jesus and his apostles. From this perspective, each teaching and each event constituted a point of intersection between heaven and earth. To believe in Jesus as the Messiah was to believe in the divine initiative in bringing the kingdom of the heavens near to earth and thus to grasp the full cost of earth's rejection of that initiative. As Jesus had said, no one except the Father had recognized the Son (11:27). That had been made clear at Golgotha when the Son had fulfilled his mission according to God's hidden ways. Once the identity of the Son became known, everything in his story became surcharged with God's own authority, power, and mercy. It became God's story as well as Jesus' story, now continuing in our story. We may call this the "ways of God" perspective.[5]

Many features in the text force readers to reckon with this perspective as basic throughout the Gospel. For instance, consider the two dramatic episodes in which a voice from heaven identified Jesus as "my Son, the Beloved" (3:17; 17:5). In the first episode, God declared God's pleasure with the repentance by which Jesus had fulfilled all righteousness. In the second, God approved the necessity of the cross for God's Son and for God's school of prophets, as a fulfillment of both the Law (Moses) and the prophets (Elijah) (see chapter 5). The storyteller thus bracketed the whole of Jesus' vocation within God's design "from the foundation of the world."

The same baseline for thinking was corroborated throughout the Gospel by citations of scripture, usually introduced by the formula "as it was spoken through the prophets." Spoken…by whom? Only one speaker is in Matthew's mind. Often these citations were statements made in the first person singular: "I desire mercy and not sacrifice"; "I will proclaim what has been hidden from the foundation of the world"; "I am the God of Abraham"; "I will strike the shepherd and the sheep will be scattered." There can be no doubt of the identity of this I. Often other personal pronouns are used, but they identify the same speaker: "*My* people…*my* house…*my* Servant," "I am sending *my* messenger," "This people honors *me* with their lips…" In Matthew's use, these texts do not serve as proofs of formal doctrines or verification of mysterious events. Rather, they are indications of a habit of thinking, a habit that is everywhere conscious of the purpose-filled presence of God, speaking through the prophets.[6]

Even more ubiquitous than these citations are the divine passives scattered through the Gospel, indicating the heavenly source of human choices: "The axe *is laid* at the root of the tree"…By whom? "The peacemakers…*will be called* the children…" "A city *built* on a mountain…" "Do not judge, so that you may not *be judged*…" "Let it *be done* for you, according to your faith…" "If I only touch his cloak, I will *be made well*…" "Take heart; your sins *are forgiven*…" "Tell no one about the vision until after the Son of Man *has been raised* from the dead." This profusion of passives provides glimpses into the inner structure of Matthew's thought-world, where the Creator's design and initiative controlled both roots and fruits of human actions. For this prophet, no less than for Paul, God was One "from whom and through whom and to whom are all things" (Rom. 11:36, au. trans.).

Such an outlook is demonstrated still further in the references to God's struggle in the heavens with God's most persistent and resourceful enemy. In scripture the first appearance of this enemy had been in the garden, when the craftiest of the wild beasts had lied to Adam and Eve and they had accepted his deception because of their desires for food, for the beautiful, and for greater knowledge. In time this serpent attracted various titles: the dragon, Leviathan, Tiamat, the devil, Satan, or simply the evil one. As soon as God had identified Jesus as God's beloved Son, Satan responded by offering him all the kingdoms of the world. When Jesus sowed the seed of God's kingdom, the devil promptly sowed the seed of his enemy kingdom (13:38–39). As God had prepared God's kingdom from the foundation of the world, God had also prepared eternal fire for the devil and the devil's angels (25:41). When God revealed the secret of the Messiah's identity, Satan immediately countered by lying to Peter about the requirements of messiahship (16:23). It was entirely logical, then, that in the disciples' prayer, the first petition should be for the coming of God's kingdom from heaven and the last petition should be for rescue from the evil one (6:13). In using this prayer, the disciples viewed every situation on earth as dependent on the outcome of that heavenly struggle.

The narrator clearly located important intersections between God's kingdom and earth's residents at points where Jesus' work extended the victory that God had won over Satan in heaven to God's subsequent victories on earth. It was the demons who first recognized such intersections at the points where Jesus proved stronger than their own Lord (8:29). The human adversaries, of course, had at hand a contrary explanation: "By the ruler of the demons he casts out the demons" (9:34). The issue was clearly joined when Jesus declared, "If it is by the Spirit of God that I cast out demons, then the kingdom of God has come to you" (12:28). He compared what had happened in his exorcisms to the success of a thief in tying up a strong man, entering his house, and plundering it (12:29). That primary victory of God, as the thief, over Satan, as the strong man, enabled Jesus to share the same authority with his disciples. When they wielded that authority, they expelled demons, healed the sick, cleansed lepers, and raised the dead (10:1–8). To Matthew and his readers, such happenings were explicable only as an earthly counterpart to the war that was also being fought and won in the heavens. Such is the war in which Matthew believed that he and his readers were engaged as he was writing and as they were reading his story.

In distinguishing these three perspectives, I have already done violence to the structure of Matthew's thought-world, in which the three are fused together. To the narrator, the entire story of Jesus was intelligible and powerful only as it reflected the hidden purposes of God from the foundation of the world and only as it was instrumental in initiating a mission that was to be continued through the school of prophets. To attempt to distill from this document data for an earthly biography of Jesus that is divorced from its heavenly roots and its later fruits is to destroy the possibility of conversation with Matthew. Unfortunately, such is the result of many current treatments of the Gospel (see p. 127ff.). The same distortion occurs when we separate study of the later mission of Jesus' students from its grounding in the design of God mediated through the vocation of Jesus. My own study runs that risk, for the center of my concern is to recover the salient aspects of their training. To minimize that risk we must at every point focus attention on the efforts of Jesus to help them understand his vocation as the source and goal of theirs, and as providing a clear revelation of the hidden course of God's creative and redemptive activity.[7]

A School for Prophets

Recognizing that caution, we will now review the evidence that the narrator had a major concern for the training of Jesus' apprentices to continue his work after his death. Readers can easily ignore this evidence when they read only small segments of the story in a disconnected fashion; it becomes impressive only when they read the entire Gospel as a unit, alert to the role of the apprentices. When they appear on stage, Peter may not always be mentioned by name.

However, when he does appear, he is a representative and spokesperson for the others. We can therefore assume that even when he is not explicitly mentioned, he is being trained along with the others.

Jesus' very first action, as he began announcing the good news of God's decision, was to call four fishermen; these would remain with him until the next to last day of his earthly mission. On Jesus' call they immediately left families and livelihoods, never to return. Like their teacher, they became homeless mendicants, journeying from town to town, relying for food and shelter on the hospitality of Galilean villagers, but subject as well to the ridicule and hostility of those same villagers (10:1–15). At the outset, the only incentive offered to them was the promise of training for a new kind of fishing. With very few exceptions,[8] Matthew limits his use of the term *disciple* to those who joined this itinerant band, elsewhere called harvesters, shepherds, teachers, prophets, or apostles. Future functions were more important than present titles. They would have primary responsibility to extend the range of his work and to care for the crowds of followers who accepted Jesus' message as that of an authorized prophet of God.

In the subsequent travels of Jesus, they accompanied him from beginning to end with only two major exceptions. They may have been absent when, in Jerusalem, Jesus was engaged in vigorous debates with his adversaries (21:23–22:45). They were surely absent from the time of their flight from Gethsemane to the meeting with him a few days later. A third possible exception may be found immediately after they were sent on their first independent field trip to the villages of Israel and when Jesus, in their absence, addressed the crowds of followers (11:1–30).

Most of Jesus' teachings were organized into substantial continuous lessons. There were five of these, and in all five these students constituted the major audience. This fact is obvious in three lessons, where the Twelve were the only listeners: In chapter 10 Jesus issued instructions to guide them in their first foray alone; in chapter 18 their future roles in governing later congregations comes into view; in chapters 23–25 he prepares them for facing critical situations after his death.[9] A fourth lecture, consisting almost entirely of parables, is addressed to a mixed audience of crowds and disciples, but even here Jesus explained the thrust of the parables to the disciples alone (chap. 13). The fifth lecture (the first in the Gospel) was the most extensive and decisive of all. Readers usually assume that it was meant for all followers. However, I will marshall the evidence that has forced me to conclude that this first "Sermon on the Mount" (chaps. 5–7) was originally intended as basic instruction for Jesus' apprentices.

In all five of these lessons the teacher combined specifications regarding the disciples' duties with warnings against dereliction in obedience. The first lecture, for example, warned against a righteousness like that of the Pharisees (5:20) and ended with warnings against building their house on sand. The manual of instructions for work in the field was punctuated with anticipations of violent public hatreds, with cautions against those who "kill the body"; if they denied their allegiance to Jesus before mortals, he would deny them before the heavenly tribunal (10:33). Often this teacher contrasted the "little faith" of his students to the great faith of a Gentile woman or a Roman centurion. From first lesson to last, the negative foil for these future leaders was provided by the present leaders of the synagogues. This fact leads a reader to suspect that the messianic judgments pronounced on the hypocrisies of those leaders were used in part for their pedagogical value. However, there were more important positive standards by which to measure the work of the future harvesters. The Messiah's work itself formed a rigorous standard; slaves must be like their master. Like his, their assignment was to bring not peace but a sword. Readers who recognized the uniqueness of the Messiah's work were reminded of the uniqueness of the work of his delegates.[10] The other standard was even more rigorous, and Jesus stated it without hesitation or qualification: They must be as perfect as their heavenly Father. And if they were to match such perfection, they must respect the otherness of God's thoughts and ways.

In making such demands of his apprentices, Jesus clearly maximized the distance between normal human conceptions of virtue and heavenly truth. He measured human thoughts and actions by distinguishing their origins: All speech comes either from the evil one or from God (5:33–37). All actions emerge either from a self-love that restricts love of others to those who love in return or from a self-humbling that loves the greatest enemy without the slightest desire for advantage. Such a self-humbling indicates one's birth as a child of the heavenly Father. The distance between the kingdom of the heavens and the kingdom of Satan is the distance between one desire and another, one impulse and another. Each disciple must remain aware of that distance.[11]

Prophetic Oxymora

In his teaching of his apostles-designate, Jesus had recourse to many apparent contradictions. For example, in his response to a rich man's difficulties in considering the requirements of discipleship, Jesus confessed that meeting the requirements was an impossibility that only God could make possible. In rhetorical terms, such an impossible possibility is labeled an oxymoron; the two things contradict each other. The gospel of Matthew is punctuated with many oxymora of this order. I have chosen some of them as titles of chapters in this book and others as epigrams for those chapters. Perhaps the greatest contradiction of all is the term *a crucified Messiah.* There are many other contradictions of the same order, based on that ultimate oxymoron: to lose life by saving it and to save life by losing it; the humiliation of the exalted and the exaltation of the humiliated; the weakness of the powerful and the power of the weakest. Contradictions of this sort seem to be intrinsic to Matthew's thought-world.

A central rhetorical reason for the use of this form is simply to call attention to the two things that contradict each other. Typical examples of the form: bittersweet, a lonely crowd, noisy silence, pride in being humble. In these simple examples, both components derive from universal experience and are explicable on that level. Matthew's oxymora, by contrast, call attention to the existence of two alternative worlds of experience. They arise out of the contrast between the earth and the heavens,[12] between human standards and divine. What is impossible *with men* is possible *with God.* The blasphemer rejected *on earth* is the Messiah appointed *in the heavens.* Those who, in his name, lose their lives on earth gain life in the heavens. These oxymora are contradictions that arise from the antithetical strategies of the two heavenly kingdoms, God's and Satan's. Minds that are controlled by human goals are opposed at every point by minds oriented by heavenly truth. There is a permanent and pervasive conflict between treasures laid up in the heavens and those invested on earth. The Gospel oxymora therefore become more than clever rhetorical devices; they are indigenous and intrinsic to a language-world in which Isaiah's axiom is accepted with total seriousness.

I now call attention to another function of the oxymora in the Gospel: They are used in order to present those who accept the message of the kingdom as antiheroes. This is another rhetorical term that is frequently applied to modern novels. Such novels choose as a protagonist someone who lacks all the attributes that would give the protagonist heroic stature. Yet as the story unfolds, readers come to recognize this protagonist as a genuine hero. Such recognition, in turn, shows how false the popular image of the hero really is. In similar fashion, Matthew presents the apostles in antiheroic roles. In the end, they themselves were forced by their teacher to discard the all-too-human yardsticks for measuring heroism.

Modern novelists also sometimes focus attention on a protagonist who is a "Christ figure," whose Christlikeness is at first hidden from all eyes except those of the omniscient narrator. When revealed as fulfilling an authentic messianic role, this protagonist places under judgment the readers' prior ideas about messiahs and messianic salvation. In rhetorical terms, Matthew presents Jesus as an anti-Messiah who destroys all competing messianic expectations (e.g., 24:5, 23–24). We will see that the education of Simon Peter proceeds, through the use of such oxymora, to disclose the otherness of God's thoughts and ways. Step by step, he was taught how to imagine the real–the real Messiah and his real heroes.

Questions for Reflection and Discussion

1. Read Isaiah 55. In what specific ways did Isaiah find God's thoughts and ways different from ours?

2. With regard to the three perspectives described in this chapter, how did Matthew find God's thoughts and ways different from ours?

3. Read again note 10. When we read this Gospel not as Jesus' biography but as the story of a group "bound together by a shared vocation," does this change our expectations of what Matthew's account might tell us? In what way?

CHAPTER 2

SALTING THE EARTH[1]

Everyone will be salted with fire.

(Mark 9:49)

After the summons issued to Peter and his fellow fishermen, the first major stage in their training appears in what is usually called the Sermon on the Mount (chaps. 5–7). We may think of this entire sermon as the induction of these fishermen into their future assignment. Because we cannot examine the whole of the address from this perspective, we have selected one statement for exploration, believing that if we grasp its wider implications, we will better grasp the multiple thrust of this opening lesson: "You are the salt of the earth." Although parallels to this declaration are found in Mark (9:49) and in Luke (14:34–35), we will refer to them only when they throw light on the Matthean imagery. We will not try to recover Jesus' own use of the metaphor or to trace the history of the saying between its use by Jesus and its incorporation into the Sermon on the Mount. Its context in that sermon provides many clues to Matthew's intention. My goal is to report on how I read the Gospel, based on the exploration of those clues.

The narrator shaped this keynote address of Jesus in full knowledge of what was to happen thereafter. He looked back from a time after the death and resurrection of Jesus and after the fulfillment

11

of many of Jesus' predictions concerning the fate of his disciples. Such knowledge was bound to color the narrative in many ways, some of which can be recovered. The first readers, as a Christian community, would listen to this story of the beginnings with knowledge of the outcomes, since their faith was grounded in the proclamation of the death and the vindication of Jesus as the Messiah. In some important sense, then, both narrator and listeners would project themselves back into the sermon and would attend with immediate and intense empathy to what Jesus had said to and about them. They would instinctively identify themselves either with the crowds or with the disciples, doing so in part because they were confronted by the same adversaries, as our study will show.

Preparation

Before the narrator had arrived at the point of reporting the sermon, he had carefully prepared the way by introducing the major participants, of whom Jesus was, of course, most important. The narrator had described how God had authorized Jesus to begin his messianic mission after he had responded to John's call to a baptism of repentance. At this baptism, God's spirit had descended on him and God's voice had identified him as God's Son. Then, victory in the long struggle with the devil had vindicated his right to employ God's power to cast out demons and to announce God's blessing on all who, like him, were humbled in heart. Jesus' authority to command was doubted neither by those present on the mountain nor by the narrator and his readers. Moreover, to accept Jesus' authority was tantamount to accepting his declarations as a disclosure of God's own designs for God's people.

Jesus' secondary audience on the mountain was evident at the outset ("When Jesus saw the crowds," 5:1) and also at the end ("the crowds were astounded at his teaching," 7:28). During the sermon, however, the crowds stood in the background. Jesus referred to them only with the vague third person plural, *they*.[2] Matthew had already pictured them with words that implied a much longer history than many readers suppose. These crowds had been attracted to Jesus during his first extended campaign in Galilee in response to his teaching, Sabbath after Sabbath, in the synagogues, his shouting of "the good news" of God's grace, his healing of many sicknesses, his power to expel demons. According to the narrator, the crowds' response had fulfilled Isaiah's promises of a light that would shine on those sitting in darkness and in death's shadow (4:15–16; Isa. 9:3–5). This fulfillment had come to people in many regions remote from Galilee: Zebulun, Naphtali, the Trans-Jordan, the way along the sea. Matthew included all the regions mentioned by Isaiah and even two others, Judea and Jerusalem. (Scholars may ask, Why these two additions? Do they suggest that the narrator may have himself been a leader in the Jerusalem churches, writing for Christians in Judea?) Coming from diverse homelands, these followers formed not one crowd but many, reflecting, perhaps, the scattered locations of churches in Matthew's day. It was clearly for the sake of these crowds, this secondary audience, that Jesus concentrated his attention not on them but on the disciples, whom he was training as future leaders. "When Jesus saw the crowds...his disciples came to him...and [he] taught them [the disciples]..." Throughout the sermon, Jesus addressed the disciples in the second person, *you,* because he was training them as future leaders of these crowds. They were *the* primary audience.

Matthew had introduced them in a capsule-sized picture of their call, in which Jesus had promised to train them as fishermen. Matthew designed Jesus' five major addresses as a training manual for these interns (chaps. 5–7, 10, 13, 18, 24–25). In this first address he almost immediately placed them in the succession of prophets (5:12), persecuted as the prophets before them had been persecuted. At the end of his story the narrator described the completion of the training (28:16–20). Throughout the Gospel, a variety of images refers to their calling as fishermen, prophets, teachers, exorcists, scribes, healers, messengers, and judges with the power to bind and to loose.[3] In all these capacities Jesus served as exemplar. In describing their role, the narrator wrote, "Blessed are you when *they* revile you and persecute you..." (5:11, au. trans.).[4] Who were these persecutors? Matthew assumes that his readers will know, but almost immediately he identifies them as the scribes and Pharisees who claim that Jesus has come to abolish the law and the prophets. *They* were the interpreters of scripture and the leaders in synagogues whose righteousness disciples must excel (5:17–20; 6:2, 5, 16). In sum, the narrator recognized the presence on the mountain of those who would remain central to the drama until the end of the Gospel: the disciples, the crowds, Jesus, and those who would prove the adversaries of all three.

The Beatitudes

The training manual began with a series of eight beatitudes in which Jesus announced God's blessing on the crowds of followers, a blessing that was phrased in the third person plural: *They* were followers described in eight different ways, though all were recipients of the same beatitude. Earlier, Jesus had announced to them "the good news of the kingdom"; now he identified them as its heirs. The setting assumes that the gift of this blessedness was something extraordinary and unexpected: God had given them a blessing that lifted the curse that the Creator had pronounced in expelling Adam from the garden. In becoming heirs of the kingdom, these beneficiaries became a single community, though their qualifications were presented in different images: They were humbled in spirit, famished for righteousness, mourners for sin, channels of mercy, spreaders of God's peace. The eighth blessing served as a climactic verification of a common merit: Their repentance induced them to accept violent hostility as the cost of following this prophet. In these declarations, Jesus spoke *about* these penitent crowds *to* his disciples. One reason for such indirection was this: Those whom Jesus had healed during his ministry prefigured those whom the disciples would heal through their own later ministries. The first eight beatitudes thus served in miniature as a photograph of the results of the Messiah's work from beginning to end, a photograph that covered as well the results of the work of the harvesters whom he would send into the same fields (9:35–38).

Modern readers often find it hard to understand why these "crowds" were persecuted. Matthew did not explain the reasons for such violent hostility against "the poor in spirit"; he could assume that his readers did not need such an explanation because they had themselves experienced it. Later readers, however, often require help in understanding it. By whom were these crowds persecuted? Surely by the scribes and Pharisees, who had rejected John's call to repentance and whose hostility to Jesus would ultimately lead to his death. What induced such violent rejection? The conviction that by his message and work Jesus was destroying the law and the prophets, the sacred scriptures of which they were the respected interpreters and guardians (5:17). Why persecute the crowds who accepted Jesus as a prophet of God's kingdom? Of what sort of people were these crowds composed? "Demoniacs, epileptics, and paralytics" (4:24). Later, these three categories were expanded to include lepers, prostitutes, the insane, the blind, deaf-mutes, tax collectors, and the recently deceased. What did these groups have in common? All were subject to forms of bondage beyond their control. Furthermore, their bondage automatically made them unclean, subject to social ostracism and barred from full participation in the life of synagogue and temple until their cleanness could be confirmed by guardians of the law. Accordingly, when Jesus expelled the demons, healed the sick, ended the various forms of bondage by declaring that because of their hunger for righteousness God had made them heirs of God's kingdom—when all this was openly declared and believed, the very existence of these "crowds" became a public denial of the authority of the scriptures and of the legitimacy of these arbiters of authority. In effect, Jesus' identification of the crowds as blessed was a blasphemous usurpation of authority and a cancellation of God's ancestral covenant with Israel.

The Succession of Prophets

In the ninth beatitude the narrator shifted his attention from the crowds to the disciples. Readers should take careful note of this transition. The eighth beatitude reads, "Blessed are those who are persecuted for righteousness' sake, for theirs is the kingdom of heaven" (5:10). The form and content of the ninth beatitude are quite different:

> Blessed are you when they revile you and persecute you and say all kinds of evil against you on my account. Be overjoyed, for your reward is great in the heavens. In that same way they persecuted the prophets who were before you. (5:11–12, au. trans.)

Apart from the common link of blessedness to persecution, the form of this ninth is obviously quite different. The eighth is a simple two-line couplet that follows exactly the pattern of the first seven. Number nine breaks away entirely from that form: a triple definition of the persecution, a command to rejoice, and a wholly new reason for such joy in the linkage of this persecution to that of the long succession of prophets. These differences in form suggest that we should treat this new beatitude not as the ninth item in the preceding series but as the first item in a new series of teachings.

In this new series it is the persecution of the disciples that is the focus of attention. Where the crowds had been persecuted "for righteousness' sake," the disciples are persecuted "on my account," that is, as my representatives or in loyalty to my assignment. They will be singled out as Jesus' spokesmen. The reward of the crowds will be to inherit the kingdom; the disciples, by contrast, will be "great in the kingdom." The clearest shift in focus appears in the identification of the disciples with the earlier prophets. This implies not only that they are themselves prophets, but also that they belong to the succession of God's spokespersons, and, possibly, that they serve as the culmination of the entire succession. It implies also that their persecutors belong to a similar succession. The narrator assumes that in the disciples' faithfulness to the Messiah's assignment they will receive the same kind of resistance from the same enemies for the same reasons as the Messiah, ample cause for them to be called great in the kingdom of the heavens.

The grouping of these disciples with the succession of persecuted prophets can be readily understood when we examine three other Matthean reports. The first, in chapter 10, describes the disciples' exploratory mission to the towns and synagogues of Galilee. Before sending them out, Jesus gives them authority to expel demons, to heal the sick, to forgive sins, and to relay the peace of the kingdom (vv. 1–15). When they go, they will be hated by all because of his name (v. 22). The Messiah assures them that in losing their lives for his sake they will save them (v. 39), and he warns them against giving way to fear. As disciples, they must be like their master (vv. 24–28). The situation in chapter 10 is simply an enlarged photograph of the tiny snapshot in the Sermon on the Mount.[5] A second enlargement comes in 24:9–14, with its predictions of torture and death, its comparisons of the fate of these slaves to the fate of their Master, its warnings against falling away, and its assurance of salvation to those who endure to the end in proclaiming the "good news of the kingdom."

The most revealing parallel to the ninth beatitude comes in chapter 23. Here the disciples, who have the power to bind and loose, are set over against the scribes and Pharisees, who earlier held such authority, but who, instead of entering the kingdom, have locked needy seekers out. The issue is seen in terms of who is qualified to sit on Moses' seat and to teach what God requires. That issue coincides with the question of whose humility is comparable to that of the Messiah (23:1–12). Jesus condemns these adversaries as belonging to the succession of those who murdered the prophets and who are now filling up the measure of that persecution (v. 31). In sharpest contrast, Jesus describes the succession of true prophets as follows:

> I will send you prophets, sages, and scribes, some of whom you will kill and crucify, and some you will flog in your synagogues and pursue from town to town, so that upon

you will come all the righteous blood shed on earth, from
the blood of righteous Abel to the blood of Zechariah…Truly
I tell you, all this will come upon this generation. (23:34–36,
au. trans.)

Here again the narrator identifies the disciples as prophets whose
work would entail persecution and martyrdom. He further includes
them within the entire succession of prophets beginning with Abel,
the prototype of all prophets (cf. Heb. 11).[6] The blood of this entire
succession is described as "all the righteous blood shed on earth";
theirs was a single martyrdom, a single sacrifice and offering to God.
The succession of prophets is matched by a single succession of
persecutors, with the faithfulness of Jesus' disciples marking a genuine
culmination of the entire story since Abel: "All this will come upon
this generation." Such is the destiny of the disciples that Matthew
had in mind in the ninth beatitude: "in the same way they persecuted
the prophets who were before you." Those words are a microscopic
summary of the macroscopic vision of the history-long drama of
bloodshed. In beginning his training of his disciples with these words,
the Master-prophet not only prefigures their future but also furnishes
the necessary clue to the meaning of the announcement that followed:
"You are the salt of the earth." That clue is the link between the
ninth beatitude and this declaration.

The Salt

Translators, editors, and printers have conspired to conceal this
linkage. Although early Greek manuscripts used no paragraph
divisions, printed Greek texts and English translations habitually
begin a new paragraph with this announcement. Misunderstanding
is further ensured when editors insert a new nonbiblical heading
between the two paragraphs, such as "Salt and Light." The separate
caption encourages preachers and teachers to begin their exposition
with this idea as something new. Doing that enables them to ignore
the controls that are exerted on the meaning of the metaphors by
their explicit linkage to these very disciples, who, as prophets, face
persecution and death. By generalizing the audience, readers break
the bond between salt and such activities as carrying the cross. This
disjunction opens the way to a high degree of trivialism and
sentimentality. If there is to be a new paragraph, it should begin
with verse 11 where Jesus begins to disclose the hazardous mission
on which the disciples are engaged. If there must be captions, I

suggest at verse 3 "Heirs of the Kingdom" and at verse 11 "Prophets of the Kingdom."

The saying about salt has become a proverb widely used in praise of anyone who makes a substantial contribution to any group. That type of interpretation is another obstacle that modern readers must overcome. Users of the proverb are often unaware of its origin with Jesus; even those who are so aware often separate the proverb from its original context in Matthew. Moreover, because it has become a familiar proverb, many assume that it was a common figure of speech even before Jesus adopted it. It is easy to suppose that its origins had something to do with the universal use of salt to season the day's food. But as I read the saying, I find it not a proverb at all. Nor is it a word of praise and commendation for meritorious service, like that offered at a party to mark the retirement of an institution's leader. Rather, the metaphor has an ominous overtone; those designated as salt are engaged in a task that leads inevitably to violent rejection. The heavenly reward is the very opposite of earthly glory, since the rejoicing is shared by the long succession of prophets whose tombs the persecutors now beautify. The declaration is a revelation of God's plan that can be realized only through the devotion of a Master-prophet and a school of prophets-designate, through whose sacrifice God's kingdom comes near: "The cup that I drink, you will drink" (20:22, paraphrased). If the disciples were to learn to drink that cup, they needed this kind of training. The God who had spoken to the Messiah, "You are my Son," was now speaking through that Son to his disciples: "You are the salt of the earth."

A warning immediately follows the salt-figure that supports this reading, a warning that is too often omitted by those who love the figure. The very length of this warning underscores its importance to Matthew. In Greek, "you are the salt of the earth" takes six words; the threat that follows takes twenty. When this threat is construed to accord with the previous reference to persecution, it can mean only one thing. Whenever disciples refuse to accept the suffering required by their vocation, the salt loses its power. It maintains its strength only so long as disciples fearlessly fulfill their assignments. Otherwise, it is thrown out (by God) as utterly useless. To think of the disciples as salt and to neglect this warning is to misunderstand. This combination of positive identification and negative warning is entirely typical of the gospel of Matthew. In a dozen instances a word announcing the unique role of the disciples is soon followed by a warning of how that role will be nullified by any refusal to bear the

cost (compare the example of Peter in 16:13–23 and in 26:31–33).
So in the Sermon on the Mount it is the prospect of prophetic suffering
that alone explains both the positive function of salt and the danger
of becoming saltless.

But there is another problem to be faced. Why was the metaphor
of salt adopted in the first place? In the daily routines of modern
readers, a primary use of salt is to season foods; in the first century
that was far from its only use. Mark reminds us of another use in his
version of the saying: "Everyone will be salted with fire [or with
salt]" (9:49). And some ancient authors add or substitute, "Every
sacrifice will be salted with salt." These forms of the proverb remind
us that salt, like fire, was essential in the temple liturgies. To be sure,
Sirach 39:26 speaks of the necessity of using salt in the kitchen, but
the temple uses were far more significant.

Among the Lord's instructions to Moses, salt was to be used in
the preparation of the incense that was to be put before "the covenant
in the tent of meeting," where it must be regarded as "pure and
holy" to the Lord (Ex. 30:34–38). Salt thus formed a part of the
atmosphere of adoration and supplication. Among the scriptural
directions for priests in preparing the grain sacrifices was this: "You
shall not omit from your grain offerings the salt of the covenant with
your God" (Lev. 2:13). Salt also was used to seal a covenant between
Aaron and the whole succession of priests: "All the holy offerings
that the Israelites present to the LORD I have given to you...as a
perpetual due; it is a covenant of salt forever before the LORD for
you and your descendants as well" (Num. 18:19). The bond of salt
also joined the whole succession of kings: "The LORD God of Israel
gave the kingship over Israel forever to David and his sons by a
covenant of salt" (2 Chr. 13:5). From these four texts one can make
the following deductions: Salt was used daily in the temple offerings
as an essential element in Israel's worship. It was a bond that united
the Lord God to both the succession of priests and the succession of
kings, and through them to the people. All generations were covered
by these bonds, all being viewed as one in their obligation to and
dependence on God. It was God who initiated the covenants of salt;
each must be fulfilled in dependence upon God. To break the bond
would carry the most terrible of consequences. These covenants of
salt were intrinsic to the entire economy of nationhood, priesthood,
kingship, worship, forgiveness of sin, national identity, and destiny.

Jesus may have been thinking of this entire panorama *before* he
said, "You are the salt..." Within this economy the image has an

immediate and significant cogency. To use the image to refer to a succession of prophets was as natural for this Master-prophet as was using it in referring to the succession of priests or kings. It is resonant with the thought of sacrificial offerings to the Lord in response to the Lord's commands and gracious gifts. These ancestral covenants provide fascinating analogies for the new covenant. A covenant of salt fuses the traditional motifs of divine judgment and redemption, curse and blessing, the memories of the entire past and the urgencies of the immediate present. Indigenous to this background is the contrast between salt and saltlessness. So when, against the background of these four texts, God says through the Messiah, "You are the salt," the speech is of covenants that bind together long successions of priests, kings, and in this instance prophets (the pronoun *you* is plural, not singular). The speech is of a divine condiment that curses and blesses, judges and redeems, wounds and heals. This is the realm within which the ninth beatitude belongs.

The Earth

But in the Sermon on the Mount, salt is only one half of a compound image, and we must look for clues to the meaning of the second half. Why is this salt the salt of the earth? At first one looks in vain for parallels to the idea of salting the earth. So incongruous is this compound that translators of the New English Bible have rejected the undoubted meaning of the word *earth* (*gē*) and have substituted the more intelligible "the salt of the *world*." This is too great a price for avoiding the linguistic awkwardness of the Greek original. That awkwardness should be conceded, but it should prompt us to look for possible explanations of the awkwardness within Matthew's own perspectives. As we have seen, the salt refers to the succession of persecuted prophets. Since there seems to be no connection between ordinary uses of salt and the earth, we should look for possible connections between persecuted prophets, the salt in this case, and the earth. And when we do that, the answer to the puzzle is at hand. We have already observed the later Matthean passage that is the photographic enlargement of the snapshot in the sermon. There the sacrifice of all the prophets since Abel is described as "all the righteous blood shed on *earth*" and the persecution of the prophets is traced to Cain, to those who shed the blood of those prophets (23:29–36). *Earth* is an important category of thought both in Matthew and in the prototypical story of Cain and Abel to which Jesus referred.[7]

And the LORD said to Cain: "Listen; your brother's blood is crying out to me from the earth! And now you are cursed from the earth, which has opened its mouth to receive your brother's blood from your hand. When you cultivate the earth, it will no longer yield to you its strength." (Gen. 4:10–12, au. trans.)

In tracing the origins of prophecy to Abel and the origins of murderous violence to Cain, early Christians took very seriously the conviction that the earth itself had been violated by all the blood shed on earth (Lk. 11:47–51; Heb. 11:4; 12:24; Jn. 8:44; 1 Jn. 3:4–17).[8] Accordingly, they took with equal seriousness the need for the earth to receive God's blessing and for the restoration of the earth to its pristine goodness. This conviction about the cursed earth may well explain why Jesus blessed the persecuted prophets as the salt of the earth. The earth needed to be cauterized and purified by their sacrificial offering of themselves. Just as God would seal a new covenant in the Messiah's blood and that blood would be an atonement for sin (26:25), so, too, the Messiah blessed disciples who would fill up the measure of all the blood shed on the earth, and thus would salt the earth (23:35–36). By loving their enemies and praying for them, they would not only become children of their Father but become perfect as God is perfect (5:43–48).[9] Salted with their blood, the earth would again become the good earth of God's creation.

Let me cite three other texts that illustrate the linkage between the persecution of prophets (the salt) and the cancellation of the earth's curse. The first is found in the epistle to the Hebrews. In chapter 11, this author presented the longest list of persecuted witnesses from Abel to Jesus himself (11:1–12:2), and through Jesus to those whose struggle against sin had not yet reached "the point of shedding your blood" (12:4). That point had been reached by "the righteous made perfect" and by Jesus, "the mediator of a new covenant" (12:23–24). Now his followers have received the blood of a sprinkling "that speaks a better word than the blood of Abel" (12:24). God spoke through that blood with a voice that shook the earth and the heaven, so that those who shared that sacrifice received a kingdom that could not be shaken.[10] No longer the earth where brother killed brother, this was an earth where brother loved brother (13:1).

A second illustration of how fearless acceptance of martyrdom transformed the earth appears in Revelation 12:

> Now have come the salvation and the power
>> and the kingdom of our God
>> and the authority of [God's] Messiah,
> for the accuser of our comrades has been thrown down,
>> who accuses them day and night before our God.
> But they have conquered him by the blood of the Lamb
>> and by the word of their testimony,
> for they did not cling to life even in the face of death.
> Rejoice then, you heavens
>> and those who dwell in them!
> But woe to the earth and the sea,
>> for the devil has come down to you with great wrath,
>> because he knows that his time is short! (12:10–12)

The self-sacrifice of these brother-prophets (Matthew's *salt*) so transformed the earth that instead of obeying the commands of the serpent, the earth came to the help of the besieged woman (12:16). The word of their testimony had transformed the earth from being an enemy of the woman and her children into being a friend and a witness to salvation (12:11). The earth no longer remained controlled by the power of the serpent, whose lies to Eve, Adam, and Cain had initiated that servitude; it had now been restored to the power of the Creator; it was again the good earth.[11]

We need not look beyond Matthew, however, for the best illustration of how the martyr's testimony transformed the very earth on which it was offered. Jesus provided this illustration when he uttered his final cry to God, having given his witness to the high priest; then the darkness at noon over the whole earth turned to light. God shook the earth, destroying the curtain in the temple, splitting the rocks, opening the tombs, so that the holy ones who had given their witness could enter the holy city.[12] In the idiom of the Sermon on the Mount, this earthquake was Matthew's way of suggesting the strength of salt, the salt of "the prophets before you," of Jesus, and of those whom Jesus would soon send out as witnesses to the same earthquake. Salt is good (as in Mark and Luke); but without its strength, salt is good for nothing!

The Light

By turning next to the metaphor of light, the narrator obviously believed that the two metaphors of Jesus were designed to reinforce each other. Although we cannot examine the light metaphor fully, we must consider it briefly because of its link to salt. The task is made more difficult because the metaphor of light involves not one but two forms of illumination: a household lamp and a city built on the top of a mountain. The two evoke somewhat different lines of thought.

When an oil lamp is lighted, if it is put under a bowl or a tub, its light is of no use to anyone, and in fact quickly goes out; this is comparable to unsalty salt. When the lamp is put on a lampstand it gives light to everyone in the house: the salt in its full strength. The lamp shining to everyone in the household (*oikia*) may have an additional nuance in that this term *household* was often used of Israel as a whole (e.g., 23:38). Prophets who fearlessly accept the hostility of their people effectively fulfill their God-given role to their people (e.g., in Mt. 27).

The narrator also spoke of the light of the *world* and not alone of the household. This is the light of a city built on a *mountain*.[13] That this unusual translation is correct is shown by the use of the term *oros,* which elsewhere in Matthew, including 5:1, is almost always translated "mountain." And because a passive voice is used for the building of this city, the narrator probably thought of God as its builder (compare Heb. 12:22). That is why the light of this city cannot be hidden. It is always possible, of course, for residents of the city to refuse to let their light shine (like the saltless salt and the lamp under a tub). But when they do let their light shine, like the light on its lampstand and the salt in its full strength, others see their good works and give glory to God, who is the source of light. The light of this city is surely linked to the ultimate origin of light, to that creative word, "Let there be light" (Gen. 1:3). The light of this city thus shines upon and through the long succession of prophets, from Abel to the martyrs at the time of Matthew's writing, turning moments of faithful witness into moments of new creation, thus fulfilling the law and the prophets (5:20).[14]

In the final chapter of this book (p. 113) we will point to the evidence that when the exalted Jesus met the disciples, he met them on the mountain where he had first appointed them—in other words, on this mountain where he had appointed them to serve as the salt of the earth. And in that final session with his apostles, their master ordered them to teach others the same commands that he had made obligatory for them. Thus, Matthew's story comes full circle, the last lesson repeating the first, with the added authority over heaven and earth that God had now given their Master. In their own obedience and in the obedience of this wider audience, the Eleven would in fact become the salt of the earth.

Questions for Reflection and Discussion

1. Study carefully the meanings in Matthew of the metaphor *earth* (see p. 20ff.) and the metaphor *mountain* (see note 13). How different are the usual meanings of these words in modern languages?

2. What is lost when the Sermon on the Mount is no longer viewed as a stenographic record of what Jesus said by one who was there? What is gained when it is viewed as cherished by a community that remembers the martyrdom of at least three of the disciples (Peter, James, John) who were with Jesus? Can the gain be greater than the loss?

CHAPTER 3

SHEEP BECOMING WOLVES

Like wolves they tear the prey, shed blood, destroy lives...Prophets have smeared whitewash on their behalf, seeing false visions. They say, "Thus says the Lord GOD," when the LORD has not spoken.

(Ezekiel 22:27–28, au. trans.)

The Sermon on the Mount should be read, as we have proposed, as an induction address in which a Master-prophet clarified the basic responsibilities that must be accepted by students in his prophetic school. In due time their work would be an extension of his work in announcing the arrival of the kingdom of the heavens and in calling for responses of repentance and faith—repentance in the form of total humility before God's judging grace and faith in the form of grateful acceptance of God's liberating forgiveness. Jesus directed these demands for righteousness specifically to this school, although they were delivered within view of the crowds of penitents who had already been freed from demonic possession and related captivities.

Thus far, we have examined only the earlier paragraphs of this lecture; now we look at the four parables at the lecture's end. Following that, we examine the ensuing panel of photographs that showed how the Master-prophet carried on his work. Finally, we study the instructions for the apprentice-prophets' first forays into the harvest field. Behind both his work and theirs, the narrator discerned the shape of a warfare in heaven between the two kingdoms, God's and Satan's. That conflict emerges on earth in the struggle between this band of prophets and the scribal authorities. For this reason, Jesus claimed that his own mission was a fulfillment of the Law and the prophets. Then he insisted that their righteousness must also be superior to that of the scribal interpreters of scripture (5:17–20). Thereafter, every teaching in the sermon served to define that righteousness, which represented nothing less than the perfection of God.

Four Parables[1]

The concluding paragraphs of this lecture contain four trenchant warnings that the master believed his students would need. Taking the form of parables, these warnings become increasingly explicit and blunt (7:13–29). He pictures two alternate gates, then two trees, two confessions, and two houses, each representing choices made under stress. Only a few apprentices would be able to pass such stringent tests. Since most would fail, the teacher gives major attention to the failures. In speaking of the alternate possibilities, Jesus mentions the negative choice second, the place of greatest emphasis: for example the wide gate, the house built on sand. Because most readers are in the habit of reading these parables as general moral platitudes addressed to any and all audiences, they must be reminded that in this case the parables contain dire warnings for a limited audience on a specific occasion.

That fact should become clear when we take note of the implications of this pointed thrust: "Beware of false prophets, who come to you in sheep's clothing but inwardly are ravenous wolves" (7:15). The opposite of *false* is *true,* as the opposite of *wolves* is *sheep.* This entire band of prophets will ultimately divide into two sets: sheep, and sheep that have become wolves. Both are said to *come to you;* that is, both are wandering preachers who are completely dependent on hosts for food and lodging, to which, as sheep, they are entitled. It is implied that both come with the credentials of prophets, making it difficult to distinguish between them, especially because the wolves can furnish very impressive credentials indeed. Such is the situation that all four parables reflect.

In this case, the false prophets can present credentials so impressive that they have deceived even themselves: "Lord, Lord, did we not prophesy in your name, and cast out demons in your name, and do many deeds of power in your name?" (7:22).

Twice they acknowledge him as their Lord, and three times they appeal to their use of his authority. In his name their campaign against demons has been amazingly successful. Surely this qualifies them to go through the narrow gate; they have produced good fruit; they have built their houses on rock. All this is very impressive. But not to their Master, not in God's eyes. Their appeal only justifies an unexpected but terrible verdict: "I never knew you! You have worked nothing but lawlessness. Get out!" (7:23, au. trans.).

Readers must ask how Jesus is able to detect these false claims. Matthew answers very simply: They have not done "the will of my Father in heaven." To Jesus that means hearing and obeying the instructions that he had given earlier in this same induction address. In their pride over their achievements in his name, they have broken those instructions. Confidence in their own power, among other things, has brought the insidious mutation from sheep into wolves. They have not fulfilled the demands of penitence and faith, but have acted for their own glory, like the scribes and Pharisees (compare 6:1–18). No doubt this total rejection by their Lord must have astonished them, as it should astonish readers.

The oxymoron of sheep's turning into wolves helps to interpret the fourth parable as Matthew understood it. Here is the familiar picture of two houses, one built on sand and the other on rock. One was built by false prophets and the other by true prophets. Both houses, like both groups of prophets, were subject to rainstorms, tornadoes, floods. Readers may infer that the intensity of the storms represented the severity of public hostility to be faced by these apprentices. They may also infer that the greater this public hostility, the fewer would enter the narrow gate, and the more likely that sheep would turn into wolves. All the prophetic apprentices in Jesus' day (as also in Matthew's) faced the same violence, the same stormy oppositions from demonic powers, both heavenly and earthly. All had listened to Jesus' clear cut-demands. The sheep obeyed; the wolves dressed as sheep did not. Few parables could more clearly declare that full obedience to this opening manifesto had become a rigorous test that would be passed by true prophets and failed by false ones.

Readers of these parables for the first time in this way must find them simply astounding. How could the Master repudiate the work of prophets who used his own authority to produce such redemptive effects? Had not Jesus himself done the same things? Would he not very soon command and authorize his messengers to do them? Did Matthew not fill subsequent chapters with case studies that used such good fruit to prove not only the operation of messianic power, but apostolic power as well? Since then, many readers have been convinced that the amazingly rapid spread of the early church was due, at least in part, to this explosion of miraculous deeds. Why, then, do these parables utter so complete a curse on these wandering prophets who called Jesus Lord? And why do these same parables announce the speedy collapse of the houses they built on sand (the congregations they established)? Instead, the Master, who would build his own house on rock, condemns them: "How great the fall!" (This adjective *great* augurs an ominous divine judgment.) Readers must ask with all seriousness why the Master-prophet so sharply rejected the work of these apprentices.

One clue might be found in the story of Jesus' own testing in the wilderness, when Satan used the most powerful of lures in the effort to persuade Jesus to rely on the same kind of miraculous signs. Another clue appears in this very induction lecture: It mentions no demand whatever on the part of Jesus that students should present credentials of this sort. Instead he required a very different sort of "miracle." When he cast out demons and healed all manner of disabilities, those whom he helped had first accepted the basic demands to repent and to believe in God's amazing new offer of God's kingdom (e.g., 4:23–24). So, too, when he first sent his harvesters into the harvest field, he instructed them to insist on the same priorities (10:3ff.). Only humble responses to God's judgment and forgiveness could make credible the kinds of deeds to which the wolves appealed. Such deeds could always be assigned to Satan's kingdom rather than to God's, as opponents proved.

Six Photographs

We turn now to examine the panel of photographs in which the narrator described Jesus' own attitudes toward his deeds of power. These may explain the harshness of his verdict. When Jesus had come down from the mountain (a symbolic descent), many crowds followed him. They recognized in him the operation of an authority from heaven very different from that of their scribes, the accredited interpreters of scripture. His first act was to respond to a leper who recognized that this authority might include the power to cleanse him of a disease that excluded him from access to synagogue and temple worship and from many social contacts as well. He believed that Jesus could cleanse him and remove these barriers. Jesus chose to do so. Hundreds of implications may be drawn from this story because of its brevity. Let me limit myself to two observations. First, Jesus immediately commanded him not to tell anyone. Various motives may be given for this command, but surely one of them must have been the desire to avoid any publicity that inevitably would distort the real source of the cleansing (compare the healing of the two blind men in 9:27–30). How different from the self-assurance of the false prophets in 7:15! As a true prophet, Jesus knew that the cleansing was due to the unexpected nearness of God's kingdom, with its promise of mercy to the helpless and hopeless. Second, Jesus took care to instruct the healed leper to further his rehabilitation with the religious community by gaining the priests' certificate for that same cleansing, so that the religious authorities, quite unaware, would be giving their testimony to the merciful presence of the kingdom. So all of Jesus' deeds of mercy became, in one way or another, signs of the kingdom's presence springing from a person's humility and faith.

The next photo is of a Roman military commander and his paralyzed slave. The most revealing line in the story is this: "I also am a man under authority" (8:9). This is clearly a reference to the military chain of command in which the centurion has received his authority from a man of higher status, and he exercises that authority over his own slave. But this authority had not enabled him to relieve the slave's paralysis. He has come to believe, however, that Jesus also stands in a similar chain of command, exercising authority received from above. This commander has conferred on Jesus the power to meet the most extreme human needs: "Only speak the word" (8:8). Thus, these few words give evidence of the faith of the soldier, faith not in Jesus alone, but ultimately in the word of the One under whom Jesus served. In reality, then, this was faith in the accessibility of God's kingdom and its gifts of mercy even to a Gentile suppliant. The commander thus declared himself to be dependent on Jesus and on his God. Such was the faith that Jesus had not found in Israel, a faith that marked this Roman enemy of Israel as a forerunner of many Gentiles whom Abraham would welcome at his table in God's kingdom. Even Jesus was amazed at this evidence of the extension of God's mercy in inspiring such faith. In this story, then, there is no hint of any self-importance or self-glorification that would contradict the truth of Jesus' wilderness tests. Rather, Matthew detected a fulfillment of the prophecy of John the Baptist (3:9). Later readers may also detect a parallel to Paul's inflammatory ideas in Romans 4.[2]

A third snapshot, a very tiny one, pictures a more intimate scene, Peter's wife's home. Here Jesus cured the mother-in-law's fever, though no special note was taken of it. The only thing mentioned was the cooking of a meal for numerous guests. On the same day Jesus cured many "with a word," presumably the word of divine authority over demons. No attention is given to the individuals who received such gifts of God; the general situation, however, enables the narrator to add an explanation of this authority over demons and sicknesses. For that explanation he appealed to what God had said through the prophet Isaiah: "He took away our weaknesses and bore our diseases" (Isa. 53:4, au. trans.). The narrator thus linked two prophets, Isaiah and Jesus, as spokesmen of the same God; more than this, he identified Jesus as Isaiah's "Servant of God" who, by being despised and rejected, had chosen to bear the burden of others' infirmities. Wounded for their transgressions, he had healed them by his own bruises (Isa. 53:3–6; 1 Peter 2:24). Matthew's audience was very familiar with Isaiah and would have been able to discern the difference between this servant and the false prophets of 7:15. This prophet healed by suffering with and for the healed.

Two other photographs may be sufficient to show the kind of model Jesus presented for his apprentices in their later ministries. The first shows Jesus at work in a clearly Gentile region, since a hog farm would have been forbidden in Israel (8:28–34). Two men had been banned from life in the town because of their apparent insanity and forced to live among the unclean tombs. In Matthew's idiom they had become the residence of many demons. When Jesus came near, the demons recognized in him the unexpected and premature intervention of God's kingdom. "Son of God, what do you have to do with us? Have you come to banish us before the time appointed?" (8:29, au. trans.). This protest implies that they had all along been expecting a day of judgment when they would face eternal banishment. Their panic showed them that such a day had come. Already the ruler of the demons had been banished from the heavens, so that their banishment on earth was an immediate sequel to that day. That gave its meaning to Jesus' command: "Go!" The insane men were freed. The demons were allowed their wish, a new residence in unclean hogs. But they had only a few moments there, because the hogs rushed into the sea—in biblical idiom, a destiny for all things evil. The story is another illustration of the same chain of command: God's victory over Satan in the heavens; Jesus' mastery over Satan on earth; the power of Jesus over the demons; the liberation of human beings from terrible suffering and even more painful ostracism. Significantly, however, there is no inclination to glorify Jesus for his power; rather, the only reaction of the nearby town was "not in my backyard," the almost universal protest to such an invasion.

The story of how Jesus healed another paralytic is highly suggestive (9:2–8). It opens a vast range of possible meanings. The story first indicates the presence of faith among the friends who carried the paralytic to Jesus. The content of their faith is not specified, but one can suppose that it constituted a joyful acceptance of the news of the kingdom's arrival. The two responses to that news as demanded by Jesus are both present: consciousness of great need and belief in the news as good. In response to that faith, Jesus immediately says, "Your sins are forgiven." (That familiar passive points to God as the one who forgives.) The response, however, provokes a sharp protest from the guardians of scripture: "Blasphemy!" Jesus then raises a key question: Which is easier, the forgiveness of sins or the healing of paralysis? To the guardians of the law the answer was clear, since they would not have violently objected to the healing, inasmuch as some of their own supporters were able to heal. But claiming authority to forgive represented blasphemy because only God can forgive sins. Any human being venturing the claim is guilty of blasphemy, a sin worthy, as was later shown, of the sentence of death.

Having stated the alternatives, Jesus proceeded to forgive the man's sins, so that these guardians might know that God had given God's authority to the Son of man on earth. As a result, the scribes became as angry as the crowds became jubilant. They gave glory, not to the Son of man, but to God for having thus brought God's kingdom within the reach of humble and believing folk.

We should not overlook one of the major implications of Jesus' words. In equating the cure of paralysis with the forgiveness of sins, he made one act accomplish what could accurately be described in two ways: forgiveness and healing. He traced that act to God's kingdom as mediated through the authority of God's prophet on earth. That one act also, by implication, treated this sin and this sickness as a single thing that was traceable to the same source and overcome by the same power.[3] In the same way, other stories identify various illnesses with demon possession and the cures with demon exorcisms. Power over demons is also occasionally described as authority to forgive sins. In this thought-world, then, two equations are accepted. On the one hand, sickness = demon possession = sin, and on the other hand, healing = demon eviction = forgiveness. All these disabilities are evils from which persons cannot free themselves by their own efforts. Then, too, these same persons suffered from both social ostracism and exclusion from religious activities; they were thus effectively barred from access to God's kingdom. Their hopes were dead. Accordingly, the possibility of healing (or freedom from demons or forgiveness) carried with it the prospect of life in a new community with a new future. Jesus' authority opened up this impossible thing as entirely possible. The enthusiasm of the crowds followed (9:8); but the greater their enthusiasm, the greater the resistance. Already, then, by Matthew's ninth chapter, this panel of pictures revealed the plot of the entire drama, from the news of God's unrestricted mercies and merciless judgment to the judicial verdict, "He is worthy of death."[4]

Four Episodes

We turn now to the more direct instruction of the disciples. To be sure, they were expected to learn from watching Jesus cope with successive situations. But Matthew was not content with such observations. The training of these prophets-to-be called for something more than a good exemplar. In four brief episodes he illustrated what would be demanded of them.

(1) When a scribe asked to enroll, he learned that he must adopt a life of homeless wandering. He must accompany and imitate a teacher who, unlike foxes, had no den and, unlike birds, had no nest. As a newscaster, the disciple, too, must find in every hostile town a host willing to risk offering him lodging and food. The narrator does not comment on the scribe's decision. Presumably he decided against such a life or more would have been made of it.

(2) When a current student requested a leave of absence so that he could fulfill his final duty to his dying father, Jesus refused. Apparently, enrollment in this school permitted no such remit from the new and hazardous vocation.

(3) A harrowing experience dramatized even more emphatically what Jesus meant by following. The disciples followed Jesus into a *boat* and they embarked together on the *sea*. These key words indicated that all the words in this episode carried both undertones and overtones, some ominous and others auspicious. As we have seen, the word *sea* carried ominous overtones as the realm proper to the powers of evil, in their resistance to the powers of God. Similar associations accompanied the picture of Jesus' traveling in a boat with these disciples (9:1; 10:2; 14:13–33; 15:39). The entire episode is introduced by a loud exclamation (*idou*) that is a virtual shout of

warning. Here the sudden intervention of an extraordinary force is announced, a shaking (*seismos*) of the sea that is called "great" (*mēgas*), a clear indication that God has engaged in a struggle with the sea by challenging the primeval powers of evil. This shaking is a premonition of other convulsions to follow: a second shaking of the sea (14:30) followed by a shaking of Jerusalem (21:10); of the heavens (24:29); of the earth (27:51, 54; 28:2); and of the soldiers guarding Jesus' tomb (28:4). In all these cases, God is assumed to be the one who does the shaking, in accordance with God's own hidden purposes. In this episode the shaking of the sea was so strong that waves covered the boat, inducing the apprenticed prophets to cry out, "We're lost! Save us, Lord!" To the Master-prophet, however, there was no crisis and no panic. In fact, he was sleeping soundly. (The words used for his sleep and his waking were the terms that later could be used for his death and resurrection.) When he awoke and gave the command, the shaking ceased, the convulsions and the calm thus corresponding to the effects of his death and vindication. The storm and the ensuing calm also corresponded to the panic of the disciples and their amazement. They had ventured to follow him even into a boat to embark on a treacherous sea, but they could not yet fully grasp the meaning of his initial beatitude: "*Blessed* are you when they *persecute* you..." Rather, their panic indicated their lack of faith: "You cowards!" Not yet could they trust God's authority over the powers of evil. Not yet could they conceive how such a terrifying storm could, at his command, turn into a calm sea, friendly to them. This episode thus provides a climax to the three basic requirements: They must voluntarily accept life as homeless vagrants, they must be willing to ignore essential filial duties, and they must, with God's help, survive the severe tests of courage when their vocation thrusts them into life-threatening storms. (Compare Ps. 107:23–32. The language of this Psalm provides the idiom for many other stories in the Gospel.)

(4) The enrollment of another disciple in the school provided the narrator with still other instructive lessons. When Jesus saw a certain customs collector sitting at his booth, he called him to follow, and the collector immediately obeyed, leaving his booth as Peter had left his fishing. Presumably this collector, named Matthew (his connection with the author of the Gospel is only a later guess), was wealthy, for most holders of that job could readily gouge the taxed and the government. At least he was able to invite to dinner not only Jesus, but his disciples and a large number of fellow workers and sinners. Readers easily understood why such collectors were

classed with sinners: They were denied standing with the loyal and faithful Israelites and therefore were unworthy of access to religious benefits. To the Pharisaic scribes it was obvious that Jesus and his disciples were made unclean by this association. Hence their question, *Why?* That question became an opportunity that Jesus seized in order to stress three revolutionary truths. The first was expressed in these two lines:

> Not the well but the sick have need of a physician...
> I was sent to call not the righteous but sinners. (9:12–13, au. trans.)

The implications should be clear. Jesus is a physician responding to orders from a commander. His instructions indicate the primary concern of this commander with the sick and the sinners; God is not concerned with the righteous and the well. All four terms–*righteous, well, sick, sinners*–are obviously used as in the languages of earth, and especially the language of earthly religion. Just as obviously, God has reversed the meaning of all four terms. It is this revolution in language that this physician-prophet has been sent to demonstrate (notice the identity of sickness and sin). Such is the first lesson that these apprentice-prophets must absorb into their own language.

A second lesson is directly related to the first. Why has God so reversed the meanings of all earthly languages? For an answer, Jesus appealed to the words of an earlier prophet: "I desire mercy, not sacrifice" (9:13). In the terms of earthly religion, all sinners were required to present sacrificial offerings. In divine terms, the only requirement was to be merciful. As a God of mercy, God required mercy and rejected all other requirements. Jesus had learned this lesson; he now ordered his disciples (and possibly the Pharisees), "Go and learn what this means" (9:13). Any doubt that Peter might have held about the meaning of this lesson would be dispelled by one of the longest of Jesus' parables. If he did not forgive a brother seventy times seven times, his heavenly father would deliver him over to be tortured (18:21–35). In due time, Peter would become the human guardian of this inflexible law of God.

The third lesson appears to have been prompted by the story of the dinner in Matthew's capacious house, the occasion for a festive celebration of that very mercy. How could there be such feasting when fasting was a far more obvious way to demonstrate the human sacrifice proper to authentic religion? Jesus' answer involves the use of a complex of biblical metaphors. Basic to this answer is the identification of Israel as the bride, with the expected Messiah as the bridegroom. The arrival of the Messiah's kingdom is the wedding. In celebration of its nearness, the bridegroom rejoices at dinner with his friends as guests. To fast on such an occasion would be unthinkable. In Jesus' view, dinners like the one in Matthew's house celebrated the coming age with its fulfillment of God's desire for mercy. It is no wonder that such behavior on the part of Jesus led to the charge, "Look, a glutton and a drunkard, a friend of tax collectors and sinners!" (11:19). Jesus saw those charges as nonsense. Because God now requires mercy and not ritual sacrifices, joy is the order of the day. This new mercy is a bolt of new cloth or a vintage of new wine that cannot be assimilated into old forms or practices (9:16–17). God's desire for mercy is so powerful that it destroys all such practices. The new has come.

After other signs had demonstrated the mercies of God for the crowds of penitents and whetted the skeptical hostility of the Pharisees, Jesus realized that there were too few harvesters to reap the abundant harvest, or, to use an alternate metaphor, there were too many lost sheep for one shepherd to find. The narrator marked this new act in the emerging drama by repeating, almost word for word, the introduction to the first act: "Then Jesus went about all the cities and villages, teaching in their synagogues, and proclaiming the good news of the kingdom, and curing every disease and every sickness" (9:35). In the first act (4:23ff.), on seeing the crowds, Jesus had begun to teach his disciples. In this new act, on seeing the crowds, he prepared to send those disciples on their first field assignment, to gather the ripe harvest.

The Authorization of Harvesters

Harvesters first required a gift of authority from the Master-prophet, so that they could also command demons and free human captives. For the first time, the number of interns is given: twelve, one for each of the tribes of Israel. For the first time, the names are listed, a list led by Peter and the other fishermen and including Matthew. These are the only ones whose former occupations are given. For the first and only time, the narrator calls them apostles, that is, messengers sent on Jesus' errand bearing his stamp of approval. His command, "Go," was essential. So, too, his definition of the task: to shout the news that God had now made accessible the powers of the heavenly kingdom, to cure the sick, to raise the dead, to cleanse the lepers, and to expel demons. Their assignment, and presumably their authority, was limited to the lost sheep of Israel, a definition of the goal that implied Jesus' vocation as chief shepherd and theirs as his under-shepherds.

This strict limitation of the field of activity is followed by strict limitations of their resources. He forbade them to take along sandals, a change of clothing, or even a staff. They could take no purse, no money. How extraordinary to assign so formidable a task among such powerful enemies and to allow them no weapons for their work. In short, they would be as helpless as he had been. Their penniless condition is reflected later in their work, when representatives of the temple who were collecting the annual tax asked Peter whether his master would pay it. The answer made clear that neither Jesus nor Peter had any money. It also made clear that, as children of their king, they were free of any such obligation. But to avoid giving offense, Jesus ordered Peter to catch a fish, to find "a coin in its mouth," and to use that to pay the tax. Whether or not he did so, we never learn. But we learn that they were free from such an obligation and that they had no money. It would seem that only in a state as humble as their master's would they be able to help others (11:25–30).

Though penniless, the apostles were forbidden to charge for their help. They could, of course, accept food and lodging, for they were completely dependent on hospitality. But generous hosts were certain to be few because of widespread hostility toward them and their work. Having listened to their announcement of God's kingdom, householders were forced to choose whether or not to invite them into their homes for meals and lodging. Those who received the apostles received the peace of God; those who denied them a welcome were threatened with a destiny worse than that of Sodom and Gomorrah. Thus, the offer of food became an important symbol of the choice faced by those who heard the news.

Hospitality posed problems for the guests as well, for the preparation and eating of food in Jewish homes was surrounded by extensive scriptural laws and by "the tradition of the elders." Pharisees took this opportunity to charge the apostles with serious infractions of both: first with ritual defilement because of their failure to wash their hands before the meal; even more serious was the sin of eating food forbidden by Moses. Jesus used those very charges to instruct the crowds concerning all possible forms of defilement. He denied that anything that entered the mouth could defile, a direct challenge to the authority of the guardians of the law. But to Peter that statement about the mouth appeared to be a parable that he could not understand, so he called for an explanation. Jesus seemed chagrined, and even shocked, that his leading apostle could not understand something so basic in his disclosure of the divine will and so inflammatory to all the lawyers. The key to the parable is Jesus' conviction that what comes out of the mouth comes out of the heart; it is the heart that is the source of all impurity. His emphasis on the heart separates his thought from that of the lawyers, and even from Peter's. So decisive is this clash over the character of all defilement that one cannot understand Jesus without comprehending his attitude toward the heart.

In the Bible the term *heart* is a code word for the control center of all desires, all loyalties, and all relationships. One finds in the heart the invisible link between the self and either God or Satan. God has a more intimate and accurate knowledge of the heart than persons themselves, for they have become experts in self-deception, as they are moved by their conflicts of interest. But they cannot deceive a God who knows every defiling impulse. Jesus finds in the heart the origin of murder, adultery, false witness, and hatred of enemies, those evils that he condemned in his induction sermon (5:21–48). Only those who love God with their whole heart, who lay up the whole of their treasures in heaven, are free from all defilement. The pure in heart are securely bonded through God to God's kingdom. No defilement comes out of their mouths; therefore, nothing entering their mouths can produce the need for sacrificial cleansing. "I desire mercy, not sacrifice."[5]

The Inevitable Conflict

Having given the Twelve authority to announce the kingdom, and having instructed them on how to find and respond to hospitality, Jesus then tries to prepare them for inevitable hostility: "See, I am sending you out like sheep into the midst of wolves; so be wise as serpents and innocent as doves. Beware of them…"(10:16–17).

This command, "See", is uttered with ominous intensity, because encounter with these wolves represents an inevitable collision between the kingdom of God and the kingdom of Satan. In this context, "See" becomes a shout of warning: "Be on your guard." Why must these sheep be as crafty as serpents? Probably because the wolves represent the serpent in the creation story; as the craftiest of animals, the serpent became the successful tempter of Adam and Eve. Why must they be as harmless and innocent as doves? Probably because, after God's first punishment of a sinful world, the dove had brought the first message of a forgiven world. As crafty as creation's primeval foe and as gentle as the first harbingers of God's peace! The earthly encounter of the sheep and the wolves will disclose the invisible heavenly encounter between the Creator and rebel creation. When the sheep understand this, they will understand how to deal with that encounter.

To be specific, when they "are dragged before governors and kings," they will have an opportunity to give their witness to God's peace. When they are "hated by all because of my name," they will have an opportunity to banish their anxiety and fear through the power of the same name. On trial and facing the verdict of death, their voices will become the voice of God's spirit, speaking through them. They will drop to the ground like sparrows but will not fall outside God's reach. Under pressure from the serpent, the doves will face only two courses of action. They can give faithful testimony to their Master; in this case he will vouch for their loyalty before his Father in the heavens. Or they can deny having ever known him (like Peter at Jesus' trial); in that case he will deny having any connection with them.

This portrait of their fieldwork can be taken, point by point, as a replica of Jesus' own fieldwork from the very beginning. In fact, Jesus drew the analogy quite forcefully. "If they have called the master of the household Beelzebul, how much more will they malign those of his household!" (10:25). Their experience in the same field will prove that as students they will be treated as cruelly as their teacher, and as slaves as unjustly as their master (10:24–25).

The Reward for Hospitality

Until its last paragraph, the fieldwork directive is concerned with the tasks of the messengers. But Jesus' instructions do not end without showing his concern for householders who, at great risk to themselves, offer hospitality to such beggars. It is obvious that these potential hosts would be unsure of the precise status and stature of their guests. A few hosts would recognize them as *prophets* with heavenly credentials. Others would accept them as *righteous,* by no means an ordinary title in Matthew's vocabulary. Still others would treat them simply as *disciples* carrying out the commands of their teacher. With regard to these three different groups, Matthew makes two important points. First, he makes clear a genuine equivalence among the three hosts: All who welcomed any guest, regardless of his assumed status, would in fact be welcoming Jesus. On welcoming Jesus, in absentia as it were, they would in fact be entertaining the One who had sent him. Thus, all three acts of generosity would bring into existence a new community, binding each host to the messenger, to his sender, and to his Sender.

There is a second point, no less significant but much less obvious. It becomes visible only when readers detect and take seriously a motif that underlies the stories and dialogues in the chapter that follows. We should notice the sequence in which the three hosts are mentioned, a sequence in terms of the assumed rank of their guests: a prophet, then a righteous man, and finally a disciple. The order appears to descend from a greater stature to a lesser one. This descending order is confirmed by two details used to describe the third. The guests are called "little ones," and to them the hosts offer a minimal gift, a cup of cold water. Yet these hosts, no less than those who offer a lavish welcome to guests with more impressive credentials, entertain both the Messiah and his Father. We should detect in this contrast and this similarity a subtle lesson. Readers, no less than actors in the drama, measure comparative statures by applying human and earthly yardsticks. Accordingly, they take it for granted that these three hosts are mentioned in descending order, from higher to lower. But Matthew follows many biblical precedents in which a sequence of three examples indicates an ascending order. To this Messiah and to the One who sent him, the least are the greatest and the lowest the highest. This reverses the usual human, earthly criteria for gauging status and stature. Here again the thoughts and ways of God are very different from those of mortals. It is this contrast that underlies much of chapter 11. As a first example, the question raised by the disciples of John the Baptist reflects the continued power of earthly criteria. "Are you the Coming One, or should we expect another?" (11:3, au. trans.). In the beginning, John had hesitated to baptize Jesus because John's demand for repentance did not seem to apply to one whom he recognized as superior to himself. Now there is a similar hesitation. The message and work of Jesus did not yet give to John convincing evidence that Jesus was the expected Messiah. First offended by the penitence of Jesus, John was now offended by the lowliness of his works, which seemed to be limited to the helpless and the hopeless, the misfits and the castoffs. For heaven's blessings to be showered only on the lowly did not correspond to John's expectations of messianic greatness.

John thus seems to have been one of the wise and competent ones from whom God had hidden the signs of blessedness that God had given to "infants" (11:25–26). God had hidden them also from the cities where Jesus' deeds of power had been done (11:20–24). The contrast between the contradictory standards of greatness became clear, however, in the astounding contrast Jesus drew between John the Baptist and "the little ones" in the kingdom of the heavens. (One should note an intentional link between the little ones in 10:42 and in 11:11.) To make the contradiction inescapable, Jesus first praised John as a prophet, then as more than a prophet, then as God's messenger sent to announce the Messiah, as Elijah himself. No one born of woman could rank above John. Yet in the kingdom of the heavens, God has reversed all such earthly standards. In the kingdom the little ones are greater! Such a reversal must be attributed to God alone. And only this Son knows God as Father. It is such knowledge that is embodied in the Son's lowliness of heart. And it is such lowliness that enables the Son to carry the burdens of the weary and the helpless (11:29). The *tapeinosis* (humbling) of Jesus in Matthew is fully congenial to Paul's view of that humbling in Philippians 2–3. It is not surprising, then, that the Messiah as God's Son should adopt God's ways of measuring greatness: The self-exalted will be humbled and the self-humbled will be exalted (11:23). This contrast between divine and human conceptions of greatness recurs in all the later chapters. John the Baptist is not the last to take offense at Jesus' understanding of the good news. And Jesus' blessing on those who take no offense in him does not prevent Simon Peter from being offended. In fact, such an offense is noted whenever Peter appears in the later story; the offense ends only when the cock crows in a belated fulfillment of Jesus' warning.[6]

Questions for Reflection and Discussion

1. In the four parables at the end of the Sermon on the Mount, Jesus was very severe with the false prophets. Why so severe? What changed these sheep into wolves? Is this severe teacher the gentle Jesus of children's stories?

2. List the major metaphors in the Sermon on the Mount. Why would Jesus and Matthew have used so many? Are some of the stories extended metaphors, for example, enabling a paralytic to walk? Can any of these metaphors be changed into literal rules?

3. Can modern apostles obey the commands of Matthew 10 today? If not, how can one change them without betraying them? How can modern spokespersons of Jesus test their own fidelity to these commands?

CHAPTER 4

SEEING THE INVISIBLE

Keep listening, but do not comprehend;
keep looking, but do not understand.

(Isaiah 6:9)

Ever since this Gospel appeared, readers have detected in chapters 16 and 17 a major turning point in the drama. Here the narrator unveils a double recognition scene. God first reveals to Peter Jesus' messiahship, and then on the mountain Peter and two of his fellow students hear the decisive announcement from heaven. This double recognition illustrates again the fusion of perspectives we have traced from the beginning. All that happened on earth could be understood only when viewed from the baseline of the approaching kingdom of the heavens.[1] Signs of that kingdom indicated an unfolding of the plan that God had in mind for God's creation from the foundation of the world. Matthew traced all human resistance to that plan to the antithetical kingdom of Satan, also located in the heavens. Whenever God sowed the seed of God's kingdom on earth, Satan responded, whether by snatching away such seed (13:19) or by sowing weeds in the same field (13:25). A variety of terms identified this enemy such as Satan, the devil, the ruler of demons, or simply the evil one. This perspective linked Satan to the primeval serpent, the craftiest of the wild beasts that

God had created (Gen. 3:1). In the various oxymora, he was usually considered the source of the earth's-eye view that was responsible for the idea of a *powerful* Messiah, in opposition to the heaven's-eye view responsible for the idea of a *crucified* Messiah. It was inevitable, therefore, that after his appointment as Messiah of God's kingdom, Jesus became the preferred target of Satan's lies. That testing began in the wilderness and did not end until the struggle in Gethsemane. By his victory, the Messiah became qualified to open the gates leading to God's kingdom in the heavens, gates that at every point were conflicted by the gates of Hades, leading to the outer darkness. The ensuing visible conflicts on earth became signs of invisible conflicts between those opposing destinies. The Messiah was sent both as a sword to incite those conflicts (10:34) and as a gatekeeper to open to earth dwellers the gates to God's kingdom.[2]

In his opening chapters, Matthew introduced readers to the heavenly components in the Messiah's vocation. The genealogy presents Jesus as the fulfillment of all the generations since Abraham, with significant emphases on the kingship of David and the deportation to Babylon. At his birth, angels celebrated his conception by the Holy Spirit as one who would fulfill God's promise through the prophets to save God's people from their sins. Born as king of the Jews, the infant immediately became the occasion for Herod's maniacal paranoia, though at the same time he was identified by wise men from the East intent on following the guiding star. Thus, the stories, miscalled "birth stories,"[3] previewed the salvation to both Israel and the Gentiles to be disclosed only in the subsequent stories. In these early stories, the chief actors were operating from a heavenly base (God, God's angels, their unwitting agents on earth, the fears of the earthly king) with no indication of any earthly awareness of what was happening.

With the coming of John the Baptist, the scene suddenly changes; now attention focuses on more witting human agents, and the ripples of earthly publicity begin to spread. In the voice of John, earlier prophets also speak. His assigned task is twofold: to announce God's heavenly action in bringing God's kingdom near to mortals and to present God's demand for repentance, obedience to which was expressed in the Jordan baptism. Jesus obeyed that demand, and in so doing chose to "fulfill all righteousness." In turn, God approved such fulfillment and declared this self-humbled Nazarene to be God's Son. In response, the Spirit drove Jesus into the wilderness and Satan began testing this baptism, this obedience, this fulfillment of righteousness, this appointment as God's Son. Each of the three tests was inherently oxymoronic in that human conceptions of God's kingdom, power, and glory were opposed to God's own design. The Messiah's rejection of all three human conceptions made possible all that followed, enabling God to fulfill through Jesus what God had promised through Isaiah: "the people who sat in darkness have seen a great light" (4:16). In his narrative, as we have noted, Matthew kept central three interlocking concerns: to tell how Jesus accomplished the vocation given to him at the Jordan, to tell how he trained harvesters to continue his vocation after Golgotha, and to tell how God fulfilled God's promise to all those "who sat in...the shadow of death" (4:16). Having already examined the interplay of these concerns in the induction address and ensuing episodes and instructions, we turn now to examine their interplay in two dialogues in 16:1–12.

In these dialogues, most readers find little of importance. This, I think, is inaccurate, for in them a discerning reader may learn not only the significance of what has happened, in heaven's view of things, but also clues to what is about to happen. Such significance is not easy to recover unless we probe beneath the surface of the narrative. The two dialogues, one between Jesus and the Pharisees and the other between Jesus and his interns, center in the oxymoron of seeing the invisible signs.

To the Pharisees...No Sign Except...

Our comments flow directly from listening to the text itself:

> The Pharisees and Sadducees came, and to test Jesus they asked him to show them a sign from heaven. He answered them, "When it is evening, you say, 'It will be fair weather, for the sky is red.' And in the morning, 'It will be stormy today, for the sky is red and threatening.' You know how to interpret the appearance of the sky, but you cannot interpret the signs of the times. An evil and adulterous generation asks for a sign, but no sign will be given to it except the sign of Jonah." Then he left them and went away. (16:1–4)

We may first ask what role these questioners play in the drama as a whole. They always appear as a group, representing a single adversarial voice. They have the function of always opposing Jesus' authority as a prophet or the authority of his apostles-designate. Within Matthew's churches, those apostles will fulfill duties parallel to the Pharisees' duties in the opposing synagogues, including that of reading and interpreting the scriptures (23:2–7). It is for this reason that the apostles-designate must exemplify a righteousness exceeding that of the scribes (5:20). So from the beginning the narrator uses these adversaries as object lessons from which their apostolic replacements should learn. Each controversy is used in such a way as to provide maximum pedagogical value in the training of the apostle-designate. Even so, this particular debate seems to add little that is new to the portrait of the Pharisees; hence, readers pass over this episode in haste to get to something new.

Much seems to justify this marginality. For one thing, there seems to be no connection to the preceding story of the wilderness supper. The Pharisees raise a single, simple question. Jesus gives a blunt answer. Exit Jesus. Again, nothing seems to link this debate to what follows. Where did these adversaries come from and where did they go? Why did they raise this question at this particular moment? What reasoning lies behind Jesus' answer, "No sign…except…"? The whole episode is remarkably incomplete. This becomes obvious if, with many ancient manuscripts, we delete the inner references to predicting the day's weather. Without them, the debate consists of a single terse question and an equally terse reply. Readers ask why. The wonderment increases when we notice that a more complete account of the same debate may be found in 12:38ff. Presumably Matthew's first readers would have recalled that episode, and in that case, this repetition seems entirely unnecessary. This fact, however, leaves unsolved the problem of why Matthew repeated the debate in this new context. Quite apart from that problem, the earlier version of the debate clarifies what Jesus meant by referring to the sign of Jonah: "The people of Nineveh will rise up at the judgment with this generation and condemn it, because they repented at the proclamation of Jonah, and see, something greater than Jonah is here" (12:41).

The first readers would surely have been familiar with the account of Jonah's arrival in Nineveh, that wicked and godless city. The prophet had been commissioned to announce the bad news: "Forty days more, and Nineveh shall be overthrown" (Jon. 3:4). But something happened that amazed Jonah. The people of this city, and even the king, believed the news and repented. Their fear of God's fierce anger induced unconditional penitence. The people demonstrated their total self-humiliation by wearing only used sacks, by sitting in ashes, and by turning from their violent and evil ways. In turn, God also repented and canceled this threat.

In Jesus' answer we should detect the most savage irony. The Ninevites had Jonah; the Pharisees have something greater than Jonah. The proclamation of Jonah was less impressive than the message of John, the message of Jesus, and the message of Jesus' apostles. Because the Pharisees surely accepted the authority of Jonah, they should now accept the fact that something greater had happened. That Nineveh, the epitome of evil, had turned from violence threw the most damning light on the refusal of Jesus' adversaries to turn from their violence. The refusal of respected defenders of Israel's status among the nations to repent was condemned by the repentance of Israel's greatest enemy! God's anger against one city was canceled; God' anger against the other, by contrast, became all the greater! No wonder that, from the beginning of the good news, the fitting message was, "The axe is laid at the root of the tree."

The reference to the ability to predict the weather belongs within this ironical climate. Those who have proved their ability to predict tomorrow's weather by reading the signs in the *sky* have proved utterly unable to detect the sign from *heaven!* The irony in this contrast becomes clearer when we note that the same Greek word is translated *sky* and *heaven.* The Pharisees are adept in reading *visible* signs from heaven (a red sun at sunset) but are blind to the *invisible* signs: the nearness of the kingdom as revealed in the action of repentance. The savagery of the irony in Jesus' answer should not, however, obscure the presence of something more than irony: If so evil a city as Nineveh had repented at the preaching of Jonah, even "this evil and adulterous generation" could do the same. If that should happen, their repentance would itself constitute the sign from heaven, the sign of the prophet Jonah, the sign that would reveal simultaneously both God's anger and God's mercy.

We return, then, to the debate in chapter 16, asking whether this clash between Jesus and the Pharisees, described so tersely by the narrator, conveyed any new meanings in this new context. These new meanings, if any, seem to inhere in the accent upon the sign from heaven, a sign that the Pharisees could not see but that for Jesus was all-important. How was this debate linked to the preceding discussion between Jesus and his disciples?

First of all, we should notice that on this occasion the Pharisees make their question about the sign a *test* of Jesus' authority. The word used for test was the same word that Satan had used in the wilderness immediately following Jesus' own repentance! Jesus needed to present a sign from heaven that he had received his authority from heaven. That test, in turn, recalled the one Israel had faced in the wilderness after God had liberated it from slavery in Egypt. Jesus had survived his trial by rejecting Satan's notions of divine deliverance. Jesus had provided a sign of messianic power by his own repentance as a fulfillment of all righteousness. In the current encounter, Jesus turns the tables on his adversaries. Would they, like the Ninevites, respond to the same sign that Jonah had given? More significantly, Jesus was preparing the ground for applying the same question to his disciples, as the next step in his training program.

In this current episode, readers may infer that the Pharisees have already failed the requirement of repentance by demanding more convincing signs than the sign of Jonah. Such a failure was especially culpable in that their sacred vocation was to interpret such prophets as Jonah and to demand the same repentance from all faithful Israelites. By rejecting the sign of Jonah and by demanding from Jesus more impressive signs than Nineveh, they had become "an evil and adulterous generation." Here the term *generation* denotes not so much those living within the same time period as those sharing the same paternity. In prophetic idiom, Israel had been a bride affianced to God. Whenever she served other gods, she became guilty of adultery. It was that long tradition that gave awesome force to Jesus' charge. This adulterous generation was also "evil," a charge that also represents the heaven's-eye view of earthly reality. Filled with evil spirits (12:46), this generation had become a "brood of vipers" (3:7; 23:32), children of the primeval serpent. Because of the refusal to repent, whores would enter the kingdom of the heavens before these adulteresses (21:31–33).[4]

The conflict ends when Jesus, the prophet, gives a dramatic sign: an abrupt departure that, as in 24:1, silently conveys the judgment of God on all who reject repentance as an adequate sign of the kingdom's nearness. The Pharisees, in their demand for a visible sign, fail the test that Jesus had passed. The subsequent stories subject the disciples to the same test–a fact that links this brief debate to both preceding and succeeding stories. In all these stories, the test centers on the ability to perceive what is hidden in penitence as a fulfillment of all righteousness and as a sign from heaven of the presence of God's power to judge and to forgive.[5]

To the Disciples...No Sign Except...

When the disciples reached the other side, they had forgotten to bring any bread. Jesus said to them, "Watch out, and beware of the yeast of the Pharisees and Sadducees." They said to one another, "It is because we have brought no bread." And becoming aware of it, Jesus said, "You of little faith, why are you talking about having no bread? Do you still not perceive? Do you not remember the five loaves for the five thousand, and how many baskets you gathered? Or the seven loaves for the four thousand, and how many baskets you gathered? How could you fail to perceive that I was not speaking about bread? Beware of the yeast of the Pharisees and Sadducees!" Then they understood that he had not told them to beware of the yeast of bread, but of the teaching of the Pharisees and Sadducees. (16:5–12)

Frequently, historians express their frustrations in recovering the past by using the wry quip, "History is a box of puzzles with a lost key." Careful readers of Matthew's entire story may well decide that such a quip applies to this incident. One puzzle, for example, is that of the disciples' bread. Why should its absence be so important? This bread is mentioned six times. Why should the bread be the occasion for such dire warnings from their teacher? Then there is the related puzzle of the Pharisees' yeast. How is the bread related to this yeast? What is the yeast, and how have the disciples become threatened by it? Both terms are obviously used as metaphors, but the force of both metaphors seems shrouded in mystery. That mystery seems to involve the bread that the disciples had fed to the wilderness crowds. The disciples appear to have misunderstood that bread, and such misunderstanding has made them vulnerable to the yeast. But how? and why? What should they have perceived in the bread?

The riddles come to focus in Jesus' climactic warning against the teaching of the Pharisees. Their earlier deficiency appears related to this danger. But the text does not mention which teaching Jesus had in mind. Is there an implicit reference here to Jesus' teaching in contrast to that of the Pharisees? Like those original students, readers are left with no clue; that is, unless clues are hidden somewhere. Within the text itself, the disciples' bread seems to be opposed to the Pharisees' yeast as Jesus' teaching is set against the Pharisees' teaching. But the disciples are confused, a confusion that Jesus attributes to their *little faith*. It is such deficiency that is disclosed in their inability to perceive what Jesus means by *bread* and by the yeast of their adversaries. As Jesus had identified those adversaries as "an evil and adulterous generation," so now he protests against the disciples' little faith. (The importance of these condemnations to Matthew seems to be indicated by the fact that they do not appear

in Mark's version of the story [Mk. 8:11–21].) The condemnation of
the disciples may be related to their lack of bread, their inability to
perceive its meaning, and their attraction to the yeast and to the
teaching of the Pharisees.

One key to these puzzles may have been revealed in the previous
dialogue with the Pharisees. It had been their lack of repentance
that had explained their fruitless request for a sign, a request that
stemmed from the yeast of their teaching. Contrariwise, heaven's
judgment of the little faith of the disciples may be explained by
deficiencies in their repentance, a fact that had become evident in
the earlier stories of the ample meals provided the crowds in the
wilderness. It was such deficiency that was the root of the attraction
of the Pharisees' yeast or teaching. This explicit reference to the
bread provided by Jesus to those crowds forces us to reread those
stories, looking for perceptions that the disciples (and perhaps the
readers) lacked.

This look back to earlier stories leads us even further than we
had supposed–to a story of faith greater than that of the disciples
(15:21–28). Jesus' commendation "great is your faith" had been
spoken to a helpless woman, a Canaanite, a resident of the region of
Tyre and Sidon. Those associations were not accidental, for the aura
attached to her identity (woman, Canaan, Tyre, Sidon) was similar
to the aura of Nineveh among Jews. The woman had appealed for
mercy to Jesus as Lord and Son of David. Her daughter had been
tormented by a demon. His interns, however, wanted Jesus to send
her away. Instead, he tested her faith by extreme provocation. When,
in response to that test, she accepted the status of a dog content with
eating crumbs from a master's table, she passed muster with Jesus.
Her total humiliation, or repentance, proved her *great* faith, unlike
the self-assurance of the Pharisees and the little faith of the disciples.

By contrast, the disciples, in their anxiety over the absence of
bread, had become vulnerable to the yeast of the Pharisees; their
anxiety, in turn, represented a misunderstanding of the crowds' bread
in the wilderness (or Jesus' teaching on that occasion). It was that
misunderstanding that allied them with the teaching of the Pharisees
(as illustrated in Jesus' previous debate with the Pharisees). They
had not yet perceived what had really happened in the wilderness
when Jesus had supplied bread to the crowds. "Do you still not
perceive? Do you not remember?…How could you fail to perceive
that I was *not* speaking about bread?" (16:9–11, emphasis is added).
Viewed from a human vantage point, that had been bread; but
viewed from Jesus' vantage point, it had been something quite

different. The failure in perception had, in fact, been a prime example of Pharisaic yeast.

In making this point, Matthew forced his first readers to reread the two stories of the crowds in the wilderness. Those two stories had ended abruptly (14:21; 15:38). No indication had been given of the crowds' reactions or even of the disciples' reactions. No hint had been provided about the source of the abundance (apart from the references to Jesus' looking to heaven and blessing the bread). The incredible multiplication attracted no public notice. If the vast surplus had a meaning, if it was a sign of anything, it was left to readers to supply their own guesses. Only in this later lesson is there any mention of the two events, and here the only hint is provided by Jesus' disappointment with the interns' lack of perception, their forgetfulness, their little faith. Only here do the wilderness meals become a clue to the puzzle of how to recognize the signs of the kingdom.

The Bread in the Wilderness

The scenes had been very dramatic. Great crowds of believers in this prophet had followed him into the wilderness, where no food was at hand. Hunger followed. In the emergency, the prophet asked his fledgling prophets to provide the needed nourishment: "You give them bread"! The disciples were unable to do so with their own meager resources, a point that Jesus stressed (five loaves for the five thousand, seven for the four thousand). However, the Master-prophet took those paltry supplies and fed the crowds, later accenting the extent of the surplus by knowing "how many baskets you gathered." Now the point of the story falls on the role of his interns—first on their inadequacy, then on their distributing the food, and finally on their filling the baskets with crumbs. All this evoked Jesus' judgment of little faith. "I was not speaking about bread!"

Interpreters may also find help from earlier incidents. One is the account of Jesus' own time in the wilderness. Driven there by the Spirit to be tested by Satan, the first test had been the possibility that by turning stones into bread he might allay his own hunger. Satan assumed that this power was Jesus' as Son of God. This assumption was probably based on the story of Israel's sojourn in the wilderness for forty years, fed by a daily gift of manna from heaven. "[God] humbled you by letting you hunger, then by feeding you with manna...in order to make you understand that one does not live by bread alone, but by every word that comes from the mouth of the LORD" (Deut. 8:3). When in the wilderness Jesus had appealed to this story of Moses, he had discerned the difference between God's manna and Satan's bread.

We should also recall Jesus' earlier instructions to his messengers when they began their first field trip. He commanded them to take along no provisions; they would receive their food from those who gave them hospitality (10:12). Should that fail, they should remember that they were of greater value to their God than many sparrows, not one of which falls to the ground without God (10:29).

In their ordination lecture, Jesus had taught the disciples to have no anxiety about food, because they could, like the birds, rely on divine sustenance. When they sought first the kingdom of God and God's righteousness, bread sufficient for the day would be provided (6:31–33). This is the confidence (and the humility) that pervades the petition in the Lord's Prayer. When they made their request for the coming of God's kingdom on earth as in heaven, that would provide the basis for asking for bread sufficient for the day (a petition for the manna from heaven?) (6:11). When they asked for bread, God would not give them a stone (7:9).

All these stories throw light on the fact that the disciples, after neglecting to provide bread, had become worried about having no bread. Such worry was indeed a sign of little faith, as heaven measured it (6:25), and a sign of being tempted by the Pharisaic yeast (e.g., the desire for a sign from heaven other than the sign of Jonah).

One might also include as background the story of the Passover meal, although the connection here is more tenuous. Both in the wilderness and at the Last Supper the bread was unleavened (in contrast to the leaven of the Pharisees). As in the wilderness, at the Last Supper Jesus took the bread, he gave thanks, he broke it, and he gave it to them. In both meals, the dialogue proceeds only among Jesus and his disciples, though in both settings their duties vis-à-vis the crowds is assumed. In both, he expected them to perceive the presence of something more than the bread: "This is my body."[6]

The scriptures had also given ominous overtones to the term *yeast*. In order to mark Israel's liberation from captivity in Egypt, God had commanded in the Passover meal the use of bread made without yeast (Ex. 12:19). By being the "bread of affliction," these loaves recalled the days of captivity (Deut. 16:3). So essential was this that "whoever eats leavened bread from the first day until the seventh day shall be cut off from Israel" (Ex. 12:15, 19). Many sacrifices in the temple required the same purity (Ex. 23:19; Lev. 2:4). Priests were ordained for service in the temple with unleavened bread (Lev. 8:26). Once a year every house had to be cleansed of its leaven. Such were the ominous overtones carried by the term *leaven* (e.g., 1 Cor. 5:6–8). Amos had accused Israel of adultery in its use of leavened bread in its sacrifices (Am. 4:1–5). All this helps to explain the potency of Jesus' warning to beware of the Pharisaic yeast. By misunderstanding the bread, his apostles-designate stood in great danger.

This review of the scriptural connotations of bread and yeast enables us to suggest a key to the related puzzles. In their anxiety over the absence of bread, Jesus' trainees proved that they had failed to remember his ordination lecture and his practitioners' guide for their first fieldwork. In their two tests in the wilderness with the crowds, they had failed to perceive how their anxiety over supplies of bread had demonstrated their "little faith." By contrast, Jesus' trust in heaven had enabled him to feed his followers generously. His brusque protest was fully justified: "Don't you see?" Their anxiety over the supply of bread, measured in human terms, ignored the available supply, measured in heavenly terms, and, in effect, transformed that bread into yeast.

When we use this key to unlock the puzzle of bread and yeast, we may perceive why this dialogue with the disciples was prefaced by the dialogue with the Pharisees. They had asked for a sign from heaven, a test that God turned back on them, proving their blindness to the sign of Jonah. In the sequel, Jesus used the bread of the wilderness feedings to show that the disciples also had failed to discern the signs of the times. It was their failure that the discussion of yeast and bread signaled. The "yeast of the Pharisees" concealed a stinging condemnation by the Messiah not only of unrepentant adversaries but of unperceiving disciples.

Such a deciphering of the code language suggests a similar key to the Messiah's warning against the *teaching* of the adversaries. The text makes this puzzle even more critical than the others: "Then they understood that he had not told them to beware of the yeast of bread but of the teaching." With that warning, this episode abruptly stops; interest seems to shift to another place and time and to another set of concerns. No clue is given to the nature of the teaching that threatened these students of Jesus. The shift in concern is as surprising as if a storyteller shouted, "Look out! A tornado!" without telling what happened next.

Here again, however, the brief debate with the Pharisees may provide helpful clues. Jesus' teaching had from the first been miniaturized in the newscast: "The kingdom of the heavens is at hand. Repent." As we have seen, that was the message of John and of Jesus, and the message assigned to his interns. Had this message, with its announcement and its demand, not been a valid word from God, the gospel of Matthew would not have been written. But this editor had made it clear that the Pharisees denied such validity. Note their challenge: "Show us a sign from heaven." Lacking any convincing sign of the kingdom's nearness, they lacked as well any inclination to repent. Jesus saw their bogus desire for a sign as marking them as an "evil and adulterous generation." The sign of Jonah (or of Peter, as son of Jonah) was wholly inadequate for them. At the outset of the Gospel preaching, they had rejected this sign (3:7–10); at the end their rejection would be even more absolute (21:28–32). Because this news and its demand were so central to his mission, it became essential for the Messiah to warn his interns against the teaching (or yeast) of the Pharisees. That teaching applied earthly human requirements to the recognition of heavenly divine activity, rather than measuring earthly events by the prophetic perception of God's purposes. The Messiah knew that at all costs his future harvesters must be trained to pass this greatest of all tests: to perceive the signs of God's kingdom. This made the issue of the *teaching* much more vital than the matter of bread or yeast.

The rest of the Gospel clarifies other reasons why the Pharisees had not recognized the signs of the kingdom. They believed that the scriptures, which they were trained to read and interpret, had specified a quite different type of sign. In fact, they had come to anticipate the kind of signs to which Satan had appealed in the testing of Jesus. Any authorized representative of the new order must produce tangible and substantial changes in the earthly fortunes of his people. He must show facility in turning stones into bread, in saving the elect from injury and death, and in establishing power over the nations. Like Satan, the scribal interpreters of Moses and the prophets had come to expect vast changes in economic, political, and religious balances of power. They could quote many passages in scripture to support such hopes of salvation. If readers had any doubts of this, the accounts of the crucifixion would prove it. If this Messiah had been truly authorized by God, he would have come down from the cross. He would have been able to save himself. If he had been God's king, God would have delivered him. It was their expertise in the scriptures, their "teaching" about the kingdom and its legitimate signs, that prevented them from perceiving its presence.

This same teaching prevented them from accepting the only sign provided by the God of John and Jesus, the sign of Jonah. Not able to recognize this sign, they felt no need to repent. In sharpest contrast to their self-confidence was the conscious helplessness of those who did repent. This latter group included a wide variety of penitents: demoniacs, paralytics, lepers, epileptics, the blind and deaf. At the very outset Matthew had assembled the various categories of these whom God had blessed by making them heirs and recipients of the kingdom: the poor in spirit, the meek, the mourners, the merciful, those famished for the bread of heaven, those persecuted because of their righteousness. In their recognition of their own helplessness, in their self-humiliation, these were the last and the lost who had laid up treasures wholly in heaven. At the outset, Jesus had redefined and re-imagined the meaning of repentance as the total self-humiliation by which he himself had fulfilled all righteousness. In the end, the same re-imagination would be demonstrated when he gave his life as "a ransom for many" (20:28). To perceive in such repentance a sign of the kingdom of the heavens would, in the end, enable these apostles-designate to perceive both the bread and the yeast.

But the story is not yet complete. After Jesus had given his brief, blunt reply to the Pharisees, Jesus departed from them and they disappeared from the scene. Now, after he had warned his students against the teaching of the Pharisees, the scene suddenly changes, without indication of the disciples' responses to his warnings. Efforts to teach them appear to have ceased. Presumably, they are still unable to grasp the truths hidden in these warnings. They have not, in fact, remembered the lessons to be drawn from the two wilderness crises by perceiving the kind of bread with which Jesus had fed the crowds. To be sure, since the narrator and his readers knew how the story would finally end, they could perceive why the apostles had such weak faith. But these apostles themselves showed no evidence of such self-knowledge.

Emerging, then, from the box of puzzles are two opposing thought complexes: the teaching of the Pharisees and the teaching of Jesus. The first involved an elusive correlation of the following: refusal to repent; inability to see the sign of the kingdom; confusion over bread; failure to understand the abundance of food in the wilderness; corruptive influence of the yeast. Each component in the complex helps readers to understand the essential pattern of thinking. The teaching of Jesus embodied an opposite correlation:

repentance; seeing the invisible; understanding of the bread and the wilderness abundance; avoidance of contamination by the yeast. Again in this case, each item throws light on the entire complex. In the former complex, one may discern human thoughts and ways that are traceable to Satan; in the latter, one may discern God's thoughts and ways, which are being mediated by the Messiah. This is precisely the issue that would face Simon Peter and his colleagues at Caesarea Philippi.

Questions for Reflection and Discussion

1. Today we do not examine the heavens except for weather forecasts. That makes it hard to understand Matthew's conception of the heavens. Does Emily Dickinson's verse help? (note 1) How many real things does Matthew locate in the heavens?

2. What did Matthew find as links between these stories: the healing of a Gentile girl, food for wilderness crowds, the disciples' arguments about having no bread, the Pharisees' demand for signs, the difference between Jesus' bread and the Pharisees' leaven? How were the disciples involved in each of them?

CHAPTER 5

MOVING THE MOUNTAIN

On that day there shall be a great shaking...
and the mountains shall be thrown down.

(Ezekiel 38:19–20)

We have now seen how carefully Matthew has stitched together a long succession of incidents. The story of the Canaanite woman provided a contrast between her strong faith and the weak faith of the disciples–a contrast, as well, between her self-humiliation and the self-righteousness of the Pharisees. The story of the disciples' inability to feed the wilderness crowds, along with their Master's success in doing so, prepared us for his remarks about their bread and the Pharisees' yeast. The story of the debate with those adversaries tied the ancient story of Jonah's mission in Nineveh to the current mission in Jerusalem. All this revealed the failure of Jesus thus far in training the disciples for their future work. Still vulnerable to the Pharisees' yeast, they did not yet see how Jesus' bread differed from theirs. So Jesus continued his pedagogical efforts, knowing that only when they understood the alternatives in the heavenly conflict between God and Satan would they be able to fulfill their mission on earth.

The Voice of God

When Jesus was again alone with his disciples, he proceeded with his examination: "Who do they say I am?"–a question rather easy to answer, for they assumed he was referring to the crowds who had followed him into the wilderness. Accepting the nearness of God's fire, these crowds had repented. They had been freed from demons and had been healed of their captivity to diverse diseases. Fed in the wilderness, they had rejoiced over God's plenty. Some of them associated Jesus with John, for when John had been imprisoned, Jesus had taken over his aborted vocation. Others saw affinities with the ancient prophets, such as Jeremiah, who had been appointed "a prophet to the nations," "to destroy and to overthrow, to build and to plant" (Jer. 1:5, 10). Still others saw in Jesus a possible Elijah, whose return was expected as the precursor to "the great and terrible day of the LORD" (Mal. 4:5). "At the appointed time, it is written, you [Elijah] are destined to calm the wrath of God...to restore the tribes of Jacob" (Sir. 48:10). The crowds agreed on one thing: Jesus spoke with "authority, and not as their scribes" (7:29).

"But who do you say...?" Jesus asked this question of all of his interns. As another example of stitching stories together, Matthew had prepared for this question earlier in Jesus' secret confession to his Father: "No one knows the Son except the Father" (11:27). When they remembered that, readers could grasp the origin of Peter's own confession. Peter could not have known Jesus as the Son unless the Father had revealed him as such. In fact, in the earlier chapters no human had identified Jesus as *Messiah,* the one appointed by God to inaugurate the kingdom of the heavens. Earlier, of course, the narrator had called Jesus the Messiah (1:1), but he had been speaking directly to the readers, who also had learned the truth. And the demons had penetrated the secret earlier; but when Jesus had ordered them not to disclose it, they had obeyed (recognizing his superior authority). Now, when the disciples were made privy to the same secret, they, too, were ordered not to tell anyone "that he was the Messiah" (16:20). That they were asked the question as a group and pledged to secrecy as a group supports the assumption that when Peter spoke, he spoke as the voice of the group (as also in 18:18–19). Because this was the first time in the Gospel that human beings recognized Jesus as the Messiah, this moment must be recognized as a major turning point in the disciples' education. Jesus' response to Peter makes that inference inescapable: "Blessed are you, Simon, son of Jonah! For flesh and blood have not revealed this to you, but my Father in the heavens" (16:17, au. trans.). The strong antithesis between *flesh and blood* and the *Father in the heavens* simply repeats Jesus' statement in 11:26. The heavenly truth is vastly more decisive than any human opinion. It establishes a more ultimate grounding for Jesus' authority than had been implied in the judgment of the crowds. The disclosure of this heavenly secret to Simon constituted God's blessing in an unlimited degree; it decisively determined his vocation. In God's plan, Simon was the son and successor to Jonah, as his mission continued that of Jonah (16:4). Because Simon's voice was that of all the apostolic interns, they, too, received the same blessing and mission: to call Nineveh (Jerusalem) to repentance. Now that God had revealed Jesus as the Messiah, what Jesus said became the Word of his Father, beginning with this very blessing of Simon. When Jesus said "You are..." the words carried weight similar to God's words at Jesus' baptism, "This is my Son," and similar, as well, to Jesus' words of ordination on the mountain: "You are the salt of the earth" (see chap. 2).

Matthew's account clearly stresses the difference between the the crowds' judgment of Jesus and Peter's identification. Their appraisals were the results of earthly denizens looking heavenward to explain the unusual aspects of a prophet's message. Peter's response was the result of hidden divine perspectives, a view of the earthly mission of the Messiah from its heavenly base. The Father's disclosure of Jesus as his Son could be made *only* from the heavens. The heavenly disclosure, however, is not limited to Simon's recognition of Jesus' Messiahship. The entire scene depicts an understanding of earthly events from the heavenly vantage point. Four times within five verses the heavens are mentioned in sharp contrast with "flesh and blood," "the gates of Hades," and things bound and loosed on earth. The disclosure of Jesus as Son carries with it the recognition of God as his Father, a recognition of God's chosen people, and of the vocation of the apostles in fulfilling God's plans for that people. In the imperious words of that Father/Son: "And I tell you, you are Peter, and on this Rock I will build my assembly[1] and the gates of Hades will not prevail against it" (16:18, au. trans.).

The person who builds this assembly speaks as Son for his Father; thus, the assembly represents the building activity of both. That assembly is built in the heavens, where it is opposed by the gates of Hades, and where God binds or looses what the apostles will bind or loose on earth. The Greek verb for *build* conveys a complex thought of building an *oikia,* a house; the promise might well be translated, "I will build my house [or assembly]." An analogous image to this house is that of the city built by God on a mountain, whose light cannot be concealed (5:14; see p. 23). Readers of Matthew would also recall the earlier parable of the man who built his house on a rock, so that wind, rain, and floods could not destroy it (7:24–25). That being true of a man-built house, how much truer of the house built by the Messiah! It surely would be able to prevail against attacks from the heavenly enemy. Such stability and security are intimated, of course, by the identification of Simon as Rock. That place where heavenly disclosure meets with apostolic recognition becomes the rock on which this Messiah will build his house.

The choice of the term *Rock* suggests a subtle but important connection between this foundation and "the stumbling block" and the rock of offense that prevent flesh and blood from recognizing the true Messiah (16:23ff.). The same image recalls numerous passages in the Psalms and prophets in which God is hailed as the Rock, with its various synonyms such as refuge, fortress, strength, redeemer, salvation. In a confession that marked the place where divine action inspired human recognition, Peter marked the boundary between damnation and salvation, as the next declaration indicates: "I will give you the keys of the kingdom of the heavens, and what you bind on earth will be bound in the heavens, and what you loose on earth will be loosed in the heavens" (16:19, au. trans.).

These words again show that this whole scene takes place on the very boundary between God's kingdom and "flesh and blood," where God reveals the points of transition between the two realms. Here the Messiah pledges himself to give to his delegates the keys to his kingdom, so that they will be able to provide access to that kingdom by freeing mortals from their captivities: expelling demons, forgiving sins, healing sicknesses, enabling the dispossessed to share in "the joys of their Lord." Their use of these keys naturally carries with it the power to exclude those whose rejection of the good news embodies the power of "the gates of Hades." Jesus' delegates are pictured standing at the doors of the Messiah's kingdom, attacked by the onslaught of the powers of evil. Here one gate is narrow indeed, as narrow as the other is broad (7:13). This picture was not snapped by a human camera, peering into distant skies; in it the Messiah was disclosing lines of conflict heretofore hidden from human vision. This conflict was not one among others in the Gospel, but a conflict being waged within and behind all the others. It disclosed the ultimate origin and the ultimate outcome of the entire drama, as the next word of the Messiah demonstrates.

The Voice of Satan

> From that time on, Jesus began to show his disciples that he must go to Jerusalem and undergo great suffering at the hands of the elders and chief priests and scribes, and be killed, and on the third day be raised. (16:21)

In this lesson, readers received a clear preview of everything that would take place. "From that time on, Jesus began…" For Jesus, though not for Peter, this disclosure from God was an intrinsic part of his Messianic vocation. "…He must go to Jerusalem…" The use of this *must* is emphatic, its implication inescapable. The Father had built this necessity into the vocation of his Messiah. Although this is the first time that Matthew has mentioned the necessity, it has been present in Jesus' consciousness from the beginning. This trip to Jerusalem is the true end of all the other travels of the Messiah, perhaps even from the first trip to Egypt (2:15). In the same sense, Peter's immediate response expressed not only the judgment of all his fellow interns but the deep, instinctive reaction of all mortals:

> Peter took him aside and began to rebuke him, saying, "God forbid it, Lord! This must never happen to you." But he turned and said to Peter, "Get behind me, Satan! You are a stumbling block to me; for you are setting your mind not on divine things but on human things." (16:22–23)

What a stunning reversal! As future keeper of the keys to the kingdom, Peter immediately succumbs to "the gates of Hades." In one breath Peter had said, "You are the Messiah"; in the next, "No, no, no!" One moment Jesus calls him blessed; the next he is Satan, setting a stumbling block for the Messiah. In essence this was the same temptation Satan had used in the wilderness (4:1–11) and would use at the end. But Jesus vindicates his Messiahship by unmasking Satan, even though Satan here speaks through the voice of Jesus' best student. The very Rock on which the Messiah would build his house becomes a potential stone of stumbling for the Messiah himself! (For other uses of this strategic verb, see Isa. 8:14; Rom. 9:33; 1 Pet. 2:8.) But on the very stone that Jesus recognized as Satan's prime test of his messianic authority, Peter, blinded by his good intentions and by universal expectations of messianic salvation, stumbles. A mind set "on human things" proves to be the tool of Satan and proof of the power of "the gates of Hades."[2] Here we are clearly dealing not with a passing moment in a long story, but a heavenly disclosure of the plot of the entire tragedy, a disclosure of the same order as one later attributed to the voice of God.[3] On the night after Jesus had sealed the covenant in his blood, God had spoken through the prophet: "I will strike the shepherd, and the sheep…will be scattered" (26:31). To the very end, then, the drama provides two answers to the question, Who wields the greater power, God or Satan? Jesus gave one answer, Peter the other. Jesus' answer validated in advance his next lesson to his interns.

The Voice of the Messiah

> If any [the context implies any *of you*] wishes to follow me, he must deny himself, take up his cross, and follow me. Whoever wishes to save his life will lose it, but whoever loses his life for my sake [as my messenger] will find it. For what will it profit one of you to gain the whole world but to forfeit your life? Or what will one of you give in exchange for your life? (16:24–26, au. trans. adapted to context)

The revelation of the living God continues in a teaching that appears many times in the gospels. Elsewhere it may seem to apply to anyone, or at least to any believer. Here there can be no doubt of its specificity. These are the words of the Son of the living God addressed only to those whom he has chosen and trained to continue his work. And his words announcing the necessity of their martyrdom immediately follow his rebuke of Peter's protest. As certainly as their Master must validate his sonship on the cross, so certainly must they take up their cross. Like teacher, like students. The necessity in their case springs from the same divine will as in his. In this context, any effort to gain the whole world would be an evasion of this necessity. If they were to choose that course, they would forfeit life as sons of the living God and as messengers from the living Lord. Satan would be as successful with them as with Peter. Readers can safely assume that the Messiah expected for his interns the same earthly enemies who had rejected him, "the elders and the chief priests and the scribes." The ultimate source of their temptation, however, would be the one he had identified: "Get behind me, Satan!" If they bargained their new life away with Satan, what would they get in exchange? Their choice would be as fateful as his. Just as the necessity facing Jesus was telescoped into a single sentence (v. 21), so the entire future of the apostles *as* apostles was telescoped into their taking up of the same cross. And as he had said in his case, "and be killed...and he raised," so, too, the necessity of their own crucifixion was followed by a promise underwritten by both the Father and the Son:

> For the Son of Man is to come with his angels in the glory of his Father, and then he will repay everyone for what has been done. Truly I tell you, there are some standing here who will not taste death before they see the Son of Man coming in his kingdom. (16:27–28)

This preview of their vocation included a final humiliation and glorification. The humiliation would be a tasting of the martyr's death, the losing of their lives for his sake. "Those standing here" clearly referred only to the twelve apostles, Jesus' only audience throughout this lesson. These martyrs would see the Son of man coming in his kingdom, in the royal power that is made perfect in weakness, to use Paul's phrase. That coming would reveal the glory of his Father and place a seal on their community with him and his holy angels. Then those who hold the keys to the kingdom would have vindicated the power of the kingdom over the gates of Hades. Thus, the Messiah would build his house (or assembly), a picture closely parallel to that described in the Epistle to the Hebrews (12:22–24). These assurances establish a firm link between the realization of the Messiah's kingdom, the cross of his apostolic witnesses, the victory of the Messiah over Satan, and God's revelation of Jesus as the Messiah.[4]

The Voice of God

The scene now changes, and the time as well. But the editor's accent falls not on such physical changes but on the Messiah's initiative in setting the stage for further instruction to three representative apostles. This new setting is well adapted to clarifying the hidden realities and the inner continuities of God's plan.

> Six days later, Jesus took with him Peter, James and John and led them to a high mountain to be alone with them. And he was transfigured before them, and his face shone like the sun, and his clothes became dazzling white. Suddenly there appeared to them Moses and Elijah, talking with him. (17:1–3, au. trans.)

One of the inner continuities in Matthew is the chain of mountains from the first mountain where Jesus had taught them that he had come to fulfill the law and the prophets (5:17) to the final period of instruction on the Mount of Olives (24–25), and then to the place where he commissioned them to go to all the nations. Perhaps one should detect an inner connection to Mount Sinai, where through Moses God had sealed his covenant with Israel. There may also be a connection with Elijah and the command, "Go out and stand on the mountain before the LORD" (1 Kings 19:11), a command that was followed by earthquake, fire, and "the sound of sheer silence" (1 Kings 19:12). That situation was one in which Israel had forsaken the covenant (1 Kings 19:10–14). Perhaps a clearer link to Elijah was provided by the tradition that this prophet had "ascended in a whirlwind into heaven" (2 Kings 2:11) as well as by the expectation that he would "come first" before the Messiah. The changes in Jesus' face and clothing were probably designed to show God's act of transfiguration, revealing the heavenly design in which Jesus shared the plan of salvation with Moses and Elijah, both of whom had been raised to heaven. This conversation in heaven indicates that both the law and the prophets have been fulfilled in Jesus as the Messiah.

The text invites readers to ask why Jesus should have chosen three apostles and why these three. The number twelve clearly refers to the twelve tribes. But why these three? The choice of Peter seems natural. He was the first fisherman to be called (4:18) and the first to be named an apostle (10:2). On other occasions as well he had been spokesman for the other apostles; in this very period of instruction he had been the one to recognize Jesus as the Messiah, and thus had been both the rock and the stone of stumbling. The churches remembered that he had become leader of the apostles and one of the first martyrs. James and John had similar credentials. They were among the first four fishermen to be called and among the first to be named apostles. With Peter they would be the apostles whom Jesus took with him to the garden to witness his final struggle with the powers of evil. More significantly, perhaps, they were the disciples whom Jesus promised would drink the same cup that he would drink (20:23). (It is likely that the promise had been fulfilled before this Gospel was written.) These three, then, were some of those "standing here" who would taste death (16:28), to whom Jesus had earlier promised the vision of the Son of man coming in his kingdom. This connection establishes an important continuity between the heavenly vision and the four oxymora in the preceding scene.

Here, as there, Peter gives the apostles' response: "Lord, it is good for us to be here; if you wish, I [or we] will make three dwellings [or tent-shrines] here, one for you, one for Moses, and one for Elijah" (17:4).

Matthew's readers had learned to view Peter's reactions with some skepticism. In the storm at sea he had shown little faith or understanding. He had needed explanations of rather obvious parables. His insight as the Rock had been followed immediately by his Satan-prompted "no, no, no." This current response reflects a similar ambivalence. "It is good for us to be here" because the purpose for this mountain meeting was surely to advance their training–no one else was present and there was no publicity following. But Peter's offer surely reflects a basic misunderstanding of that purpose, even though neither Jesus nor God replies to Peter's offer within the ambiance of the vision. Readers, however, are left to wonder what was wrong with this notion of building three shrines in honor of the three heaven dwellers. Was the eternal heaven the place for an earthly tent? Or was it wrong to build such shrines? Did this desire substitute reverence for obedience, a way of succumbing to the yeast of the Pharisees, who were famous for commemorating prophets who were safely dead (23:29–30)? Was Peter still illustrating Satan's power to deceive (16:22)? Was he conscious, perhaps, of God's transcendent purposes but not ready to accept the cost? Whatever may be the truth, Peter's words drop into an immense void; they are wholly incongruous in this heavenly scene.

When the same celestial cloud enveloped the three apostles, they heard a voice from the cloud:

> "This is my Son, the Beloved; with him I am well pleased; listen to him!" When the disciples heard this, they fell to the ground and were overcome by fear. But Jesus came and touched them, saying, "Get up and do not be afraid." (17:5–7)

These are Jesus' only words in this episode, spoken after the epiphany is over. The only words spoken within the ambiance of the vision were those of the Father. Both the words of the Father and those of the Son indicate that the chief objective of the heavenly visitation is the training of these disciples for their later work. They were the only ones addressed by the voice from the cloud. With only one addition, those words of the Father were the same words that had been spoken from a cloud at the baptism of Jesus (3:17). That addition is the emphatic command, "Listen to him!" In the Gospels the word "to listen" (*akouete*) often means "to obey." This celestial setting, then, gives to that heavenly command the awesome support of Moses and Elijah.

The words that follow, however, do not sufficiently explain what this listening or obedience involves. To what words of Jesus were they to listen? When we realize that this entire epiphany should be seen as an insert into the story of Jesus' efforts to train his apostles, we discover a possible explanation. The theophanic inset with its final command to listen provides the highest conceivable degree of verification to the earlier interlocked teachings. In his forthcoming trip to Jerusalem, Jesus would fulfill his messianic vocation (16:21). Those who listened to him would share his cross (16:24, 25). Should they try to avoid martyrdom, they would lose their lives. Some of them would be martyred and save their lives; this would not happen, however, until or before they saw the Son of man coming in the kingdom. In manifesting his glory and power through this beloved Son and his faithful apostles, God would demonstrate God's victory over "the gates of Hades" and would share with them the keys to God's kingdom. These apostles would *listen* to God by obeying these teachings of Jesus. It is entirely fitting, therefore, that the story of the mountaintop vision should end with the words, "When they looked up, they saw no one except Jesus himself alone" (17:8). Entirely fitting, also, is the fact that they told no one about the vision. When they had come down from the mountain, they could return to the conversation that the disciples had been having with Jesus before he and the three had withdrawn to the mountain. He had been telling them that if they continued to follow him they would lose their lives and that, before that happened, they would see him coming in his kingdom.

That is the promise that now prompted them to ask, "Why, then, do the scribes say that Elijah must come first?" (17:10). Perhaps this question was framed in such a way as to imply their continuing attraction to the teaching of the Pharisaic scribes (see p. 47f.). That may be; however, the question implied that fulfillment of his prediction of the coming of the Son of man would be postponed until after the coming of Elijah. His answer immediately dispensed with such a postponement of his prediction.

The Voice of the Son of Man

"It is indeed true that Elijah must come first to restore all things. But I tell you, Elijah has already come. The scribes, however, did not recognize him and did to him as they wanted to do"...Then the disciples knew that he was telling them about John the Baptist. (17:11–13, au. trans.)

Here the narrator referred to other places in which he had identified Elijah with John (11:12, 13). Also, the narrator would later identify the scribes with the leaders in Jerusalem who had rejected John (21:32). Having dealt with one possible appeal to a delay in the fulfillment of his promise, Jesus then dealt with another: "So also the Son of Man is about to suffer at their hands" (17:12). Here the Messiah declared that the very prediction against which Peter had protested so vigorously in the preceding lesson would be fulfilled very soon at the hands of the same scribes that had rejected John. This pending death would then automatically activate the prospect predicted for them: They would face the necessity of cross-bearing. Some of them would lose their lives for his sake, but they would not die before they saw him coming in his kingdom (16:28). The vision of heaven in which Moses and Elijah talked with Jesus provided the assurance that this expectation would also come true. Small wonder that the only words of Jesus spoken to them on the mountain were these: "Do not be afraid." The nearer they were to Jesus' passion, the nearer to their own.

The Examination

Thus far we have examined the multiple thrusts of the decisive lesson taught by this messianic teacher to his messianic delegates. That lesson had been introduced by the story of wilderness food, by the delegates' misunderstanding of the bread, and by their vulnerability to the teachings of the Pharisees and Sadducees. The same lesson had received its heavenly imprimatur from the conversations of the Messiah with Moses and Elijah, and from the voice from the cloud. Now, after teacher and class had come down from the mountain, they rejoined the crowd with its urgent needs. Here the crowd became the classroom in which the interns were examined on the degree of their understanding of the previous lesson.

The examination format may escape unwary readers until they are alerted to the multiple correspondences and contrasts that connect the lesson and the examination. The account of the examination resonates with the account of the lesson in many ways. In one we are introduced to a father who loves his epileptic son, who is hopelessly in bondage to a demon; in the lesson we learned of a father and his beloved son, who was destined to cast Satan from his heavenly throne. The suffering of one son was a bond to the suffering of the other son, though in one case the suffering marked the power of the demon and in the other case the suffering marked the defeat of the whole demonic realm. Both cases of suffering were described in a way that suggested its terrible depth and its universal range. In both it is made clear that each father suffers with his son. The suffering of one son is mentioned immediately after the prediction of the suffering of the Son of man, suggesting a possible correlation between the Messiah's suffering at the hands of the scribes and the other son's suffering at the hands of a seemingly all-powerful demon.

This resonance adds great poignancy to the statement of the one father: I brought my boy to your disciples, and they could not heal him (17:16). The failure of the disciples in this examination proves their failure to understand the previous lesson. They did not yet have the power on earth to bind this demon and to release its prisoner. They had not yet accepted the absolute interdependence of God's identification of Jesus as the Messiah with the necessity for that Messiah to suffer, or the interdependence of the Messiah's suffering and their own. Not having received the power over Satan in heaven, they had not yet received power over this demon on earth. "They could not heal him."

The contrast between the students and their teacher was immediately demonstrated. The teacher ordered the boy to be brought to him. He rebuked the demon; it left the boy; the epilepsy was healed instantly. Jesus' success made all the more blatant their failure, though it also raised serious questions about his own failure as a teacher of the previous lesson. The whole story reached its natural climax first in the question of the disciples, "Why couldn't we do that?" and then in their rebuke by the teacher, a rebuke even more stinging in its implications than his rebuke of the demon. We must look closely then at his rebuke and his response to their embarrassment.

His rebuke took the form of two exclamations: "How much longer must I be with you?" "How much longer must I put up with you?" (17:17). Readers should be able to explain these exclamations, and it is natural that interpretations will vary widely. All inferences must be drawn with great hesitation and stated with great tentativeness. For me, the rebukes do not express petulance or anger or the inclination to abandon these students. Rather they seem to voice disappointment and deep sadness. It would seem that Jesus had hoped for a clearer grasp of his teaching, but he now realized that such a grasp would require a much longer period than he had expected. I infer also that a chief purpose of his mission from the very beginning had been the training of these Twelve and that he had hoped to complete this training before his death. Now that he expected that death very soon, their obtuseness made it increasingly doubtful whether such a hope would be realized. "How much longer must I be with you?" Not much longer, and perhaps not long enough! There is also the implication that their dullness has become a component of his suffering, his personal anguish, his aloneness in a hostile world, his sense of failing to complete his Father's mission. "How much longer must I *endure* your failure to understand?"

Now we must weigh the meaning hidden within Jesus' answers to the disciples' question, Why? "Your little faith." You are a "faithless and perverse generation" (17:17). In this accusation of "little faith" we hear an echo of several earlier episodes. Early on, there had been the incident of a sudden storm when their boat had been about to be swamped while he was asleep, and they had panicked: "Why are you afraid, you of little faith?" (8:26). Later had come another emergency on the water, when he had come to them walking on the water. On that occasion Peter, confident of Jesus' authority, had begun to walk on the water, but his faith had failed when a sudden squall struck him. Jesus had saved him, but only in order to rebuke him for his lack of faith (14:22–32). Most recently, Jesus had chided the disciples for their failure to understand the two wilderness emergencies, when their inability to feed the crowds had been overcome by his own ability (16:5–12). Their inability to heal this man's son was a precise parallel to these earlier instances of little faith. Most recently, of course, their lack of faith was simply their failure to understand Jesus' four interlocking teachings in the preceding lesson.

A "perverse generation"! This accusation adds several nuances to the charge of little faith. The verb translated "perverse" appears in the passive, leading one to ask who perverted this generation. Who had misled them? One answer is most probable: the same power that had induced Peter to deny that the Messiah must suffer and be crucified (16:22). They had been led astray by the primeval deceiver. This, I think, is also the force of the noun "generation." The apostles in training who have been led astray belong to a single generation in that they share a common paternity, the devil himself.

Although Jesus thus provided this terse and accurate answer to the question of *why,* there is no indication that the editor or his readers magnified the guilt of the apostles-designate. They would have understood too well the power of the world (the "human things" of

16:23). The power of Satan to deceive was so extensive that, within the sphere of worldly thinking, a Messiah crucified could be nothing but an anti-Messiah, and his cross-bearers could be nothing but anti-heroes. Any kingdom formed by the union of a crucified Messiah and his crucified apostles could be nothing but an antikingdom. Any God who required his Messiah and apostles to die could be nothing but an antigod, whose grace in atoning for sin would be too costly to be welcomed as grace. Only a disclosure of heaven's view of the struggle between the Messiah and Satan could make sense of such reversals in human wisdom and power.

It is important to note that this examination of his interns did not lead their teacher to recrimination beyond the judgment of little faith, severe as that judgment was. Rather, it led him to give a surprising encouragement.

> Amen, I tell you,[5] if you have faith no larger than a mustard seed, you will be able to say to this mountain, "Move from here to there," and it will move; and nothing will be impossible for you. (17:20–21, au. trans.)

This promise implies that a shifting of the mountain is as yet impossible for these interns of "little faith." In a word, then, this oxymoron summarizes all the impossible possibilities in the narratives of these two chapters. The impossibility inheres in their attraction to the teachings of the Pharisees and their misunderstanding of the bread provided by their master. But just as all things are possible to God, the Messiah now makes the grain of mustard seed accessible to them (compare 13:31–32) and with it the moving of the mountain. In the thinking of those whose baseline is the earth, such power is impossible; in the thinking of those whose baseline has become the kingdom of the heavens, it is possible.

Questions for Reflection and Discussion

1. According to Matthew, God revealed Jesus as God's Son four times: 3:17; 16:17; 17:5; 28:18. How similar are these? How different? Together do the four serve as summaries of the Gospel? In what way?

2. On two of these occasions, Satan tries to twist the meaning of these revelations. What was his strongest argument?

3. Christians have always found it hard to define the word *faith*. If you examine the occasions when Jesus charged his "prophets" with "little faith," what inferences can you draw concerning the meaning of faith?

CHAPTER 6

WEAKNESS RELEASING POWER

Listen, you that are deaf;
*   and you that are blind, look up, and see!*
Who is blind but my servant,
*   or deaf like my messenger whom I send?*

(Isaiah 42:18–19)

The metaphor of a tiny seed's moving a massive mountain is so incongruous as to require investigation. Jesus must have adopted it because of its very incredibility. In the setting just examined, Jesus used it in condemning the lack of faith of his interns by contrast to the faith of the epileptic's father. That radical contrast proves that these interns, even after the mountaintop disclosure, did not yet fathom the interlocking oxymora of a crucified messiah and his cross-bearing delegates, who would lose their lives by saving them and save their lives by losing them. How tiny a mustard seed! How immovable this mountain!

The implicit truth is much the same as that conveyed by the risen Lord to Paul near the beginning of his mission to the Gentiles: "My grace is sufficient for you, for power is made perfect in weakness" (2 Cor. 12:9). It was that grace that enabled Paul, in his campaign among the Gentiles, to endure maximum weakness (a weakness defined by insults and persecutions) because he discovered in that helplessness "the power of Christ." The risen Lord was entitled to announce this truth because of the power released in his own weakness when he endured the utter humiliation of Golgotha. In this apocalyptic reversal of all earthly wisdom, the power of his Father was disclosed.

For many readers, the force of that oxymoron, however, is greatly diluted by the earlier stories of messianic power displayed in his miraculous ability to heal the sick and to cast out demons. The flaunting of such abilities seems to belie any attribution of this messianic power to any weakness on his part. By contravening the laws of nature, those "deeds of power" seem to contradict the genuineness of claims that he became "last of all." We must therefore examine this miracle-working power, asking how it was revealed in messianic weakness.

The Stories of Group Healings

The relevant texts fall into two groups, those in which attention focuses upon groups and those where it focuses on individuals. In the first category are ten texts:

1.	4:23–24	6.	12:15
2.	8:16–17	7.	14:14
3.	9:36	8.	14:34–36
4.	10:8	9.	15:30
5.	11:5	10.	15:32–39

In these ten, the narrator mentions a wide range of human needs and disabilities: leprosy, paralysis, sin, blindness, deafness, inability to speak, hunger, lameness, poverty, possession by demons, death. Modern readers usually find it difficult to see any common factor in such a list. We tend to group together medical cases, separating them from psychological abnormalities, and distinguishing both from economic stress and religious needs. To understand this narrator, then, we must first ask why he treated all these forms of weakness the same.

One answer is given by the very first summary (numbers 1, 3, and 4). All these groups are united by the fact that they are responding to Jesus as he teaches in their synagogues and proclaims "the good news of the kingdom." The gist of that news had been summarized earlier in the words of John and would be summarized later in the words of the apostles: "Repent, for the kingdom of the heavens has come near" (3:2, au. trans.). It is in their response to this message that the sick are healed. Such a response included repentance for sin, for with the approach of the kingdom comes God's judgment: "the ax is lying at the root of the trees" (3:10). The act of self-humbling before God made the news good indeed: the curing of every disability among the penitent. These cures became signs of God's grace, available to all who accepted the gift of God's kingdom.

The grounding of all these stories in the reality of God's grace explains why such diverse needs are mentioned together. Any distinction between paralysis and sin disappears when the forgiveness of a paralytic's sin simultaneously frees him from paralysis (8:2–8). The distinction between demon possession and other maladies evaporates when not only insanity and epilepsy are attributed to demons but also such inactive ailments as blindness and muteness. Jesus identifies the bread with which he fed hungry multitudes in the desert with his teaching, in sharp contrast to the leaven of the Pharisees (see p. 50). When poverty is associated with leprosy, and teaching with food for the hungry, and blindness with the power of demons, we move into a realm where a special language is operating. Here diseases are not to be defined by reference to a medical chart. Poverty is not to be located by consulting sociological analyses of class structure. In this realm the terms draw their primary meanings from God's understanding of the human condition. To enter this realm, readers must consult the dictionary of terms provided by the prophets and the Psalms. For example, Matthew draws many of his images of dereliction from Isaiah, as is shown by the following citations: Isaiah 6:9–10//Matthew 10:14–15; Isaiah 9:1–2//Matthew 4:15–16; Isaiah 42:1–4//Matthew 12:18–21; Isaiah 53:4//Matthew 8:17; Isaiah 56:7//Matthew 21:13–14; Isaiah 62:11//Matthew 21:5. Matthew and Isaiah spoke the same language.

Scattered throughout the Gospel, readers find many descriptions of these beneficiaries of Jesus' cures that supplement the medical or psychological prognoses. Those who are healed are people sitting in darkness and in the shadow of death. They are worn out from carrying heavy burdens, as required by the law. In Isaiah's poetic images, they are bruised reeds and guttering wicks. Demon-possessed, they cannot free themselves; sinners, they cannot forgive themselves; blind, they cannot find their way; paralyzed, they cannot walk; dead, their weakness has become total. All texts agree on one thing: their acceptance of the good news, announced by a stranger from Nazareth, in whom they "take no offense"; and that makes all the difference.

Their actual status before their cures is described clearly by Jesus when he finds that their numbers are so great as to require more harvesters: "When he saw the crowds, he had compassion for them, because they were harassed and helpless, like sheep without a shepherd" (number 3). This identification as *sheep* comes immediately after the Pharisees have accused Jesus of casting out demons through the authority given to him by the ruler of the demons and immediately before he gave his interns the authority over demons. That double context, before and after, explains the thrust of this image. It is the heavenly shepherd who has claimed these harassed earthlings as his heavenly flock. These sheep are harassed by the Pharisees and helpless in meeting their standards of righteousness; these shepherds exclude them from God's flock. Few animals are more completely at the mercy of predators than sheep without a shepherd. In this case, the shepherds have rejected them; as interpreters of the law sitting "on Moses' seat...they tie up heavy burdens, hard to bear, and lay them on the shoulders of others; but they themselves are unwilling to lift a finger to move them" (23: 2–4). Making demands on these sheep that are impossible to meet, these shepherds lock them out of the kingdom of the heavens. "You do not go in yourselves, and when others are going in, you stop them"(23:14). Jesus' scathing attack on these self-confident shepherds is prompted by his compassion for the "sinful" sheep they have abandoned.[1] Their attack on him is prompted by their conviction that he is not qualified to open the door to the kingdom and that these sheep are not qualified to enter it.

If we are to understand Jesus' "deeds of power," then we must chart the lines of struggle between these competing shepherds and their two flocks. The shepherds are distinguished by their understandings of the location of the door to God's kingdom and by their authority to define the conditions of entrance. The Pharisees are offended both by Jesus' role as shepherd and by those whom he welcomes into God's kingdom. The group of penitents whom Jesus heals are not offended by him (number 5). When we respect those battle lines we can understand various aspects of the so-called miracles.

For example, these stories often stress the fact that "*all* were healed." Casual reading may induce the assumption that the reason for accenting this *all* is to maximize the miraculous power wielded by Jesus. On the contrary, the purpose is to stress the sharp division between the two flocks and the two shepherds. The kingdom of

God welcomes *all* who repent and believe. All the sheep whom former shepherds have shut out of the kingdom are now welcomed by the new shepherds, whether John, Jesus, or Jesus' interns. To this narrator then, there is only one great miracle, God's gracious opening of the kingdom to *all* who repent and believe. Faith in that gift is the mustard seed. The cure of "*every* disease and *every* sickness among the people" is simply the assurance that God's promise is reliable.

When we examine the first of this group of texts we find that, immediately after describing the range of diseases that are cured, the narrator describes the same crowds in other terms. They are the "poor in spirit," the mourners, the meek, the hungry for righteousness, the persecuted, the forgiving...All these receive God's blessing. And that blessedness takes the form of life within the kingdom of the heavens (5:1–10). Each of these things—the sickness, the penitence, the blessings, life in the kingdom—can be expressed in many different images, but there is only one great miracle: the release of God's gracious power to human weaklings.

The Stories of Individual Healings

Matthew tells fourteen stories in which Jesus brings specific individuals within the range of the kingdom mercies:

1.	8:1–4	a leper
2.	8:5–13	a centurion's paralyzed servant
3.	8:14–15	the fever of Peter's mother-in-law
4.	8:28–32	two Gadarene demoniacs
5.	9:2–8	a paralyzed man
6.	9:18–26	the deceased daughter of a synagogue leader
7.	9:20–22	a woman with a hemorrhage
8.	9:27–31	two blind men
9.	9:32–34	a demoniac unable to speak
10.	12:9–13	a sabbath worshiper with a withered hand
11.	12:22–23	a blind and mute demoniac
12.	15:21–28	a Canaanite woman's demoniac daughter
13.	17:14–18	a man's epileptic, demoniac son
14.	20:29–34	two blind men

As one looks for common features in these stories, several things become clear. For instance, in no case is the recipient of a cure named; there seems to be no interest in the identity of the person. In no case is the earlier life described except to indicate the status in society and the severity of the ailment. Nor is the later life described except to show the reality of the cure. There is no suggestion of later membership in the church. Even more surprising, in only rare cases does the person healed show an immediate reaction to Jesus' help. Instead of describing the joy of those who are healed, the thought shifts to the reactions of the crowds or to the false explanations by the adversaries. Usually, however, the narrator is content to describe the former helplessness, the request for help, and the act of mercy.

In virtually every story, the presence of faith is important, whether explicitly or implicitly (e.g., number 7). In one case, the absence of a cure is explained by the lack of faith (13:57). In more than a third of the cases, this faith is attributed not to the one who is sick, whether demon-possessed or paralyzed, but to others–a father, a mother, friends, a servant's master. This distinguishes these stories from many healing accounts in other cultures, in which an individual's own trust in the charismatic powers of a famous healer is sufficient to produce a cure. Again this feature points to the grounding of Jesus' deeds in the advent of God's kingdom, in fulfillment of God's age-long promises to Israel.

In Matthew's selection of believers in the kingdom, there are fathers and mothers, daughters and sons. Special significance attaches to several of these believers. One is a Roman military officer, concerned for the sickness of his servant. A man *under* authority, he recognizes Jesus as another such man, who has a source of help with greater authority. Matthew uses such faith to proclaim judgment upon the lack of faith in Israel (number 2). Remembering the conflict between Jesus and the Pharisees, the appeal of a synagogue leader on the occasion of his daughter's death is quite amazing. Told and retold in situations where many synagogues were hostile, this appeal would have carried many overtones (number 6).

In still another instance, the reality of desperate physical need appears to become secondary to other factors; that is, the meeting near Tyre and Sidon between Jesus and a Canaanite woman, which to Jews would trigger the memories of earlier wars with Canaanites. In fact, Jesus does not allow anyone to forget the vast distance between her status and that of "the lost sheep of the house of Israel" (number 12). In total humiliation, however, the pagan mother accepts that cruel distinction. For the sake of her daughter she is willing to accept the position of a Gentile dog, begging for crumbs from a Jewish master's table. Such humility is clearly evidence of great faith, which Jesus asks God to recognize: "Let it be *done*." Because of the mother's faith, the daughter *is healed.* That these two passives refer to God's power is shown by the crowds' response: "They praised the God *of Israel*" (15:31). God's glory, Jesus' mercy, the mother's faith, the daughter's helplessness—these converge in the defeat of the demon and the healing of the daughter. It is typical of these stories, then, that they express faith in the authority of Jesus and simultaneously in the source of that authority in God. "They glorified God, who had given such authority to human beings" (number 5).

One of the strangest features of the stories is this: None of the bystanders raised doubts about the actuality of the cure. It is taken for granted that the paralytic could walk and the blind men could see. The only debate is over the source of Jesus' authority. To be sure, everyone assumes that the authority came from heaven, but in several cases (e.g., numbers 5, 9, 10, 11), Jesus' adversaries trace his authority to the kingdom of Satan rather than to the kingdom of God.

This makes urgent the question of how the recipients of Jesus' mercies viewed his relation to heaven. At the outset of his mission, Jesus simply announced the advent of the kingdom and called for repentance and belief in that kingdom. Such belief included, of course, reliance on Jesus' right to speak for that kingdom. It was commonly assumed that such right to speak for God belonged only to prophets. In the story of Jesus' visit to Nazareth, the dearth of deeds of mercy is explained in this way: "Prophets are not without honor except in their own country and in their own house" (13:57). Jesus also associated his own power with that of Jonah and John the Baptist (11:9; 21:26). His decision to share his own authority with the Twelve carries the same implication (10:41). When Jesus asked for the views of the crowds about him, the only analogies suggested were prophets: John, Elijah, Jeremiah, "or one of the prophets." And when he entered Jerusalem for the final appeal to his people, his followers chanted: "This is the prophet Jesus from Nazareth in Galilee" (21:11). Such an explanation of the source of his authority seems to have been adequate. Only in a rare instance did a cure lead bystanders to pose the question, "Can this be the Son of David?" (number 11). That question, however, was immediately answered in the negative by the Pharisees.

The identification of Jesus as a prophet has one strategic exception. When the healing required the eviction of demons and when these demons were permitted to speak, they recognized Jesus as "the Son of God" who received power "to torment us before the time" (number 4). As the earthly agents of Satan, they have special access to knowledge that already "before the time" God has overcome the kingdom of Satan.

This same conviction is expressed by Jesus himself in his answer to the charge that the source of his authority is Satan: "If it is by the Spirit of God that I cast out demons, then the kingdom of God has come to you" (12:28). This single statement implies five links in the descending chain of authority: the kingdom in the heavens where God rules, the Spirit of God with its power, Jesus with authority to use this power, the demons who heretofore have been immune to that power, and the demoniac who has been summoned to repentance and trust in God's kingdom. We may infer that all five links are operative in each exorcism. Later on in the same story, Jesus clarifies the relation of the first three links in that chain (God, Spirit, himself). Freedom from Satan's power requires acceptance of the role of the Spirit of God, but it is compatible with rejection of his own role as the Son of man (12:32). In this case, of course, faith in Jesus links the demoniac to faith in the Spirit and thus to the power of God's kingdom. But Jesus warns that those whom he (as Son of man) frees from demons remain vulnerable to even more terrible captivity (12:43–45).[2] He has already warned his messengers that pride in their own power as exorcists immediately cancels their link to his authority (7:22–23). The gate to the kingdom remains narrow even for those with power to exorcise demons, and not alone for those who have been healed.

The Faith of Jesus' Interns

Thus far I have dealt with all the healing stories except two, which require separate treatment because they fulfill a different function. Earlier stories focused on the faith of those needing help, a faith that the healer could recognize. In these two stories, although the same features are present, attention shifts to the *lack* of faith on the part of those whom Jesus has selected as future healers and whom he has been training for that role from the beginning.

When he edited the traditions about Jesus, Matthew recognized two significant facts about those reports. The first is this: Although the roster of exorcisms and cures is extensive, there is no recounting of any cure by Jesus of his interns. They have been pictured as traveling with Jesus and learning from his teaching and example how they would best execute their later tasks. Like his, theirs will be a work of healing, though there is no instance of their curing a sick or blind person within the Gospel itself. Like him, it seems, they have no need to be healed.

This may explain a second surprise. In the stories that describe two sets of actors, the healed and the prophets-in-training, the faith of the first group is in sharp contrast to the lack of faith of the second. Those who are healed are often the least likely prospects: a Canaanite "dog," a Roman commander, a synagogue leader. With faith, healing; without faith, no healing. Against this background, Matthew reports that five times Jesus rebuked his trainees with the words, "You of little faith" (6:30; 8:26; 14:31; 16:8; 17:20). Why this sharp contrast? It would seem that healers needed faith with a higher potency. Captives of demons could be freed by faith in an exorcist, whether Jesus or one of the Pharisees. Exorcists, by contrast, must have faith grounded in their own victory over demons, and, since demons on earth are subject to the authority of their heavenly ruler, exorcists must demonstrate power over that ruler. Only that victory enables them to free others.

The two healing stories that are designed to underscore the absence of faith on the part of the Twelve are both placed after those interns should have learned the source of such authority. They come after Peter has recognized Jesus as the Son of God, after he has been rebuked for accepting Satan's lies, and after God, in the presence of Moses and Elijah, has ordered three disciples to hear and obey God's Son. In the first of these stories (number 13), when Jesus learns that they could not expel a demon, he brands them as a "faithless and perverted generation" (see p. 67). He fully expected them to have faith sufficient for this challenge and was deeply disturbed by its absence. It was perhaps this disappointment that prompted him to announce for the second time that he would soon be betrayed "into human hands." His requirement "faith the size of a mustard seed..." described a condition they could not yet fulfill.

The final healing story in the Gospel (number 14) expresses another condemnation of their lack of faith, although such a divine judgment remains implicit. Jesus has just announced for the third time what would happen in Jerusalem in the coming days. He even gave in greater detail the nature of the cup that he would drink. Then he asked James and John if they were able to drink the same cup. Their *yes* rang false. They did not yet grasp what that cup signified, how it would totally reverse all human calculations of weakness and power. And they wholly misjudged their own abilities. Their blindness, not yet healed, illuminates the faith of the two blind men who cry, "Lord, have mercy on us, Son of David" (20:30). When Jesus touched their eyes, these beggars regained their sight and followed him to Jerusalem, presumably joining the crowds who welcomed "the king of Zion" riding on a donkey. Their plea, "Let our eyes be opened," pronounced harsh judgment on the disciples' proud, "Lord, we are able."

All these healing stories may be read in very different ways. Many readers construe them simply as episodes in the life of Jesus, materials for a quite unique biography. Or they can be construed as lessons in a training manual in which a Master-prophet prepared his prophetic successors to deal with key adversaries in a shared mission. Those adversaries would not be enemies of flesh and blood but "spiritual forces of evil in the heavenly places," to use the terms of Ephesians 6:12. Therefore, those lessons had to clarify potential resources for defeating those heavenly adversaries. This second construal becomes quite essential in reading five other stories that at first seem to exalt Jesus' power over nonhuman nature but are really designed as tests of his successors' faith. Twice the testing takes place in a wilderness, twice in a boat at sea, and once in the shadow of the temple. In all five, attention focuses on the training by the Master of his interns in their struggle with these unseen but real enemies.

We have already examined the use of the wilderness as a place of testing. In the Bible, a wilderness is not so much a place on the map as a place of danger, where human beings are helpless and alone without resources of their own, where they must wage hand-to-hand combat with the panoply of evil forces. Just as Matthew links Capernaum to Sodom and views all the prophets as a single generation opposed by a single generation of their enemies, so he thought of all wildernesses as a single site for all trials. It was there that Satan used Jesus' hunger as a powerful lure; there that Israel, on its initial escape from captivity, had survived only with the gift of the bread of heaven. So, in two successive wildernesses, the Twelve registered their own disobedience of Jesus' command, "You must not be anxious for food." In these wildernesses he makes them responsible for feeding the crowds of his followers. Their anxiety, in sharpest contrast to his confidence, demonstrates their lack of faith. They had been deceived by the leaven of the Pharisees and had failed to grasp Jesus' teaching. Not yet were they qualified to replace him as shepherd of these sheep by providing them with their food "in due season" (24:45, au. trans.) (see p. 47).

Even more clearly than the wilderness, the sea was viewed as home for evil forces and, therefore, as a place to test the stamina of these interns. They were especially vulnerable in a boat during sudden, unexpected squalls. In both of these storm stories, the only persons present are the interns, their teacher, and the heavenly powers embodied in the winds and waves. For this situation the Psalm provides a preview that was well known to any faithful Jew.

> For he commanded and raised the stormy wind,
>> which lifted up the waves of the sea.
> They mounted up to heaven, they went down to the depths;
>> their courage melted away in their calamity;
> they reeled and staggered like drunkards,
>> and were at their wits' end. (Ps. 107:25–27)

The same Psalm describes the deliverance by the Lord:

> Then they cried to the LORD in their trouble,
>> and he brought them out from their distress;
> he made the storm be still,
>> and the waves of the sea were hushed. (107:28–29)

In the first of these storm stories, the Lord had just stressed the demand for total sacrifice on the part of disciples. When they followed him into the boat, that embarkation dramatized their acceptance. Soon the winds, however, became so strong that waves were swamping the boat–a backdrop for a scene in the foreground, where the teacher was sound asleep while they were "at their wits' end." But when they in terror awakened him, his first rebuke was addressed to them: "Why are you afraid?" His second rebuke, addressed to the storm, produced "a dead calm." It would be difficult to imagine a sharper image of the relationship of teacher, students, and enemies (see p. 32f.).

In the second storm at sea, several new features are added (14:22–33). Now Jesus commands them to embark without him, thus forcing them to face the storm without him. They soon find themselves far from land, battered by high waves, helpless in making headway against a contrary wind. On this occasion, they see him, not asleep this time, but coming toward them at the heart of the storm. Now, it is his presence there that at first terrifies them. Only his words, "It is I," can calm their fears.   *I am*

Those words give Peter sufficient courage to ask his Lord to command him to "come to you on the water." Receiving and obeying this command, this representative apostle shows progress in his own mastery of the waves, until he notices the force of the wind. Then his fears take command. Of all the wonder stories, this is one of the most transparent in showing how these apostles, in their personal battles with the evil forces, reveal first their lack of faith and then their discovery of Jesus' presence at the heart of their strongest fears. Their confession of him as "Son of God" emerges when they discover him at the epicenter of the storms that obedience to him provokes. Not yet, however, even in making that confession, do they exhibit the faith that he demands. He still condemns their little faith. It could not be otherwise in following one who is most present when most hidden by storms.

Finally, we must look at the story in which Jesus disclosed messianic power by cursing a fig tree, a word that was effective at once. The fig tree is a familiar image for God's people in Israel, a fig tree from which God expected fruit. The basic drama is outlined by Jeremiah: "This people [is] turned away in perpetual backsliding…" "No one repents of wickedness…" "The false pen of the scribes has made [the law of the Lord] into a lie…" "From prophet to priest everyone deals falsely…" "When I wanted to gather them, says the LORD, there are no grapes on the vine, nor figs on the *fig tree;* even the leaves are *withered* " (Jer 8:5, 6, 8, 10, 13, emphasis added).

Matthew locates his edition of this prophecy at a most significant moment, immediately following the visit to the temple when Jesus expels those who have made God's house a den of robbers and where, at the same time, he heals the blind and lame. In this context the fruitless fig tree clearly refers to that temple. Less directly the story echoes other descriptions of Israel's perfidy: "the city that kills the prophets" (23:37), the Pharisees who prevent others from entering the kingdom (23:13), the massive buildings of the temple whose stones will be thrown down (24:1–2), the vineyard workers who seize and kill the messengers from the owner of the vineyard (21:33–44).

In this version of the story, then, the judgment on the fig tree is spoken only to those being trained for their mission to this same Israel. And it is told to them, not in order to display Jesus' power over trees and not in order to vent his anger at the temple robbers, but as the basis for a promise made to these trainees. They will need to remember this promise when they enter the same temple, when they call the vineyard workers to repentance, when they face the overwhelming power of these massive buildings. When they later become convinced of his victory over these same adversaries, they will be able to grasp the terms of their own victory:

> "Truly I tell you, if you have faith and do not doubt [in the parallel version of the promise: have faith as small as a mustard seed], not only will you do what has been done to the fig tree, but even if you say to this mountain, 'Be lifted up and thrown into the sea,' it will be done." (21:21–22)

That, however, is only a promise, though offered with the greatest confidence. Not yet has the condition, the *if*, been fulfilled. In fact, Matthew does not present these men as having faith at any time before Jesus' passion. In fact, it is only in parables that their faith is mentioned, and that becomes possible only after his resurrection.

> "Who then is the *faithful* and wise slave, whom his master has put in charge of his household, to give the other slaves their allowance of food at the proper time? Blessed is that slave whom his master will find at work when he arrives." (24:45–46, emphasis added)

The faithful slave will be one who has learned from his master's death the heavenly source of his power.[3] In the account of the crucifixion, the jeers of the chief priests, scribes, and elders disclosed heaven's secret. "He saved others; he cannot save himself" (27:42). Jesus was able to save others *because* he could not save himself. It was through his weakness that God proclaimed justice and victory to the Gentiles (12:18).

Questions for Reflection and Discussion

1. Comparing the texts from Isaiah and Matthew as listed on page 71, test the accuracy of the statement that the two writers spoke the same language.

2. How convincing do you find the explanation of Jesus' cursing of the fig tree? What would serve as a better explanation, and how might that explanation serve as a promise Jesus makes to his prophets?

3. In note 3, George Steiner, a Jew who is a professor of Comparative Literature at Oxford University, suggests an explanation of Jesus' "miracle-working power." Do you agree or disagree with his explanation? Why? Why not?

CHAPTER 7

LOSING LIFE BY SAVING IT

The heart is devious above all else;
it is perverse—
who can understand it?

(Jeremiah 17:9)

Jesus' efforts in the training of his interns reached dramatic intensity as he became aware of the approaching arrest: "How much longer am I to be with you?" Such intensity also grew in proportion to the growing failure of the Twelve to imagine what was happening and in proportion to his bafflement over their obtuseness. The more he attempted to penetrate their defenses, the more they resisted comprehension.[1] In chapter 26, Matthew describes in detail this growing impasse. I urge readers to examine that chapter carefully to make their own discoveries before I present the evidence as I see it.

The Parable

In chapter 25 the final parable discloses the judgments Jesus would make of his disciples' behavior following his death. When he reported this parable, one that is found only in this Gospel, Matthew completed a cycle of parables, all of which, in a quite specific way, focused on the disciples' future behavior. This last parable visualized

83

situations when believers had encountered such persecution as he had described in chapter 10. They would face hunger, nakedness, sickness, expulsions, trials before councils and courts. Would the apostles then accept the risks that would result from feeding the hungry, providing refuge for the refugees, and visiting brothers in prison? The dangers would make them forget all his promises of praise or blame ("When did we *see?*…When did we not *see?*"). But their conduct would determine on whose side they were fighting in the heavenly war. Unwittingly they were choosing either "the kingdom prepared for you…" or "the eternal fire prepared for the devil…" Their shepherd was also a royal judge whose verdict would be either "come to me…" or "depart from me…" As one who had become last of all, this judge would weigh their treatment of "the least of these, my brothers." The parable was highly relevant to his task of preparing them for the immediate future, after his arrest, when, except for Peter, they would refuse to visit him in prison.

Episode One: The Other Simon (26:1–13)

That preparation begins with two warnings. First, he reminded them for the third time that he must die and for the first time made the date specific—"after two days." That date could not have been more significant; it was Passover. Second, the narrator supported Jesus' announcement by reporting the conspiracy to arrest and kill him. There is no inkling that the interns knew of this plot, though, of course, it was no secret to Matthew's readers.

They would easily detect the silent irony in the next incident. Such irony was embedded in its location: the home of Simon the leper, an outcast whose uncleanness barred him from offering sacrifices in the temple and who made others unclean by coming into contact with them. His name reminded readers of Simon the Rock, whose denial of suffering for the Messiah had been the voice of Satan. This author used personal names for the minor characters so seldom that, when he did so, it was for good reason. He does, to be sure, name the members of the Nazareth family, the prophet who baptized Jesus, Caiaphas, Pilate, and the women at the tomb. But with few exceptions, the minor characters remain nameless. One exception is Jesus Barabbas, so named in order to accentuate the choice made by public outcry at the trial. A second exception is Simon from Cyrene, who was compelled to carry the cross that Simon from Galilee refused to carry. A third exception is this leper who, on the eve of Passover, generously furnished food and lodging for these thirteen pilgrims from Galilee. Alert readers can hardly miss the damning judgment implicit in the names.

In the leper's house, another judgment emerges in the unexpected appearance of an unknown and unnamed woman who angered the prophets-in-training by wasting precious ointment on Jesus' head. She appears out of nowhere and then disappears, but her generosity condemns their stinginess. More important, she unknowingly announces the coming Passover sacrifice and thus condemns those who had been repeatedly warned of it. Still, they refused to face the date of Jesus' burial that her good deed anticipated.

Episode Two: The Passover Curse

> Then one of the twelve, who was called Judas Iscariot, went to the chief priests and said, "What will you give me if I betray him to you?" They paid him thirty pieces of silver. And from that moment he began to look for an opportunity to betray him. (26:14–16)

Just as the action of the woman gave tragic depth to the supper in the leper's house, so, too, the covenant sealed by Judas with the priests added profound pathos to the next supper, when Jesus sealed his covenant with his students. Their teacher made very clear the character of this occasion: "My time is near; I will keep the Passover…with my disciples" (26:18).

In reading this story, modern readers must overcome a silent temptation, that is, to read it as the initial instance of a Christian sacrament and not as a climactic instance of the Jewish festival. A further handicap is to concentrate only on that fragment of the story that is most familiar: the words of institution. Lectionary and liturgical habits tend to separate these words from their extensive narrative setting. Matthew designed his account of the Passover so that it would be read as an unbroken whole. For him and his first readers this narrative recalled long and rich traditions of passover celebrations, beginning with God's freeing God's people from their Egyptian bondage. Each Passover marked the solemn renewal on the part of both God and Israel of this ancient covenant. According to this Gospel, Jesus had limited his earlier work to Israel and had instructed God's messengers to go only to Israel. This supper brought that joint mission to a conclusion, with vivid reminders of its successes and failures; those reminders, in turn, could now be seen against the background of a long history of abject slaveries and miraculous deliverances. Each item in the liturgy would call to mind God's demands and Israel's rejections. The house must be cleansed of all leaven. The sacrificial lamb must be unblemished. The lamb's blood is a sign of deliverance to slaves and of death to their captors. Each meal must be eaten with staff in hand, sandals on feet, and clothing readied for a hasty departure. The whole occasion was "a festival to the LORD" and "a day of remembrance for you" (Ex. 12:14). Matthew's repeated phrase, "while they were eating," provided ample time for such remembrance and celebration. For purposes of analysis, we have divided the entire narrative into three segments, which must all be considered parts of a single story: the passover curse, the passover promise, and the passover sequel.

The tragic dimensions of the curse are suggested by the symbol of these thirteen celebrants eating from a common bowl. When they dipped their hands into that bowl, they accepted strong covenantal bonds. As their last meal together before the teacher's self-sacrifice, it represented his last chance to help them understand themselves. So his first words to those who had shared food from the common bowl were these: "Truly I tell you, one of you will betray me" (26:21). In response, all of them joined in specious claims to innocence: "Surely not I, Lord" (26:22). In their common disavowal, Judas becomes their spokesman no less than Peter had been on earlier occasions. The common bowl was their bond; by dipping into it, they had both accepted and betrayed that bond. The teacher knew that such betrayal was a fulfillment of God's design: "It is written…" He also knew that such necessity only increased their responsibility: "better not to have been born…" That curse expressed not human anger but messianic awareness of the source of betrayal in the invisible warfare between two opposing kingdoms. Before the evening was over, their betrayals and denials would signify Satan's power while his faithfulness would represent God's power. By surrendering to Satan's deceptions, they had become even more culpable than the priests, because only they had shared the common bowl.[2]

Episode Three: The Passover Promise

> While they were eating, Jesus took a loaf of bread, and after blessing it he broke it, gave it to the disciples, and said, "Take, eat; this is my body." Then he took a cup, and after giving thanks he gave it to them, saying, "Drink from it, all of you;

for this is my blood of the covenant, which is poured out for many for the forgiveness of sins. I tell you, I will never again drink of this fruit of the vine until that day when I drink it new with you in my Father's kingdom." (26:26–29)

In this second part of the conversation at the table, Jesus continues to speak to all the students, and to them alone. The first part had concentrated on their words and actions and had cast a somber light on their hearts. This part now casts a luminous beam on his words and actions: "He took...blessed...broke...took...gave." The commands–"Take; eat; drink"–are addressed only to the Twelve and to all of them, including Judas and Peter. In eating this bread they now eat his body; in drinking this wine they now drink his blood. They accept their part in this double covenant with him. Except at one point, every word of Jesus' deals exclusively with their present and future relation to him: The blood is poured out for *many* for the forgiveness of sins. His blood spells forgiveness for many, but he seals this covenant only with the Twelve. Readers should recall that in the earlier chapters, whenever Matthew had referred to the necessity that the Son of man suffer, he had insisted on the same necessity for them. Most recently, immediately before his final approach to Jerusalem, Jesus had assured James and John that they would drink the cup that he drank, though it was clear that at that time they were not ready to drink it. Clearly, then, at the passover supper, when Jesus said, "This *is* my blood...which is poured out," the reference was to the next day's sacrifice (as was true also of the cup in 26:39).

Jesus clearly addresses the final words to the Twelve. Never again would he drink wine until that day when he would drink with them anew...in his Father's kingdom. These words had meaning only to them, and only on that final evening. These words leave no place for repeated earthly observances of the supper; they are excluded by the flat "Never again." Here there is no room for regular repetitions of the sacrament "in remembrance of me." We must not import into this narrative our memories of the other gospels. Here all attention is focused on "that day when..." Jesus linked the final announcement of the nearness of his death to the pledge of a reunion with them in the kingdom of his Father. At no point has he relaxed the rigor of his commands, nor has he granted any extenuating circumstances for their blindness and betrayals, yet he includes them all in the promise of reunion "on that day."

Matthew's first readers were bound to ask, What day is that? When will it come? Do the earlier chapters provide answers? They do. That day comes when they drink his cup. When they vindicate their own prophetic mission by belatedly following him; that is, by taking and bearing his cross. By drinking that cup Jesus receives his Father's authority to seal this covenant with them. When they drink the same cup, their deaths will proclaim the same victory over Satan as did his death. Through this narrow door, they will enter into the power and glory of his Father's kingdom. The passover promise is thus a final variant of an earlier assurance: "Truly I tell you [the familiar messianic edict], there are some standing here [only the disciples] who will not taste death before they see the Son of Man coming in his kingdom" (16:28). The confidence with which the betrayed and denied teacher issues this promise to his be-fuddled students intensifies the terror, the pathos, the intolerable contradictions in that supper conversation. Such a pledge, sealed by bread and wine, is a virtual reenactment of all the earlier oxymora of the Gospel. It is a pity that so few modern celebrants of the sacrament are fully conscious of the savage irony, the bitter realism, the abysmal depths in Matthew's story. Their Master gives this binding pledge to the disciples knowing that they will, before the night is over, deny that they ever knew him. Having accepted the covenant to share his broken body and poured-out blood, they now accept his promise of reunion in his Father's kingdom, even though within hours their actions will prove an unworthiness that, humanly speaking, is unforgivable. What treachery! On his part, what confidence![3]

Episode Four: The Passover Sequel

When they had sung the hymn, they went out to the Mount of Olives. Then Jesus said to them, "You will all become deserters because of me this night; for it is written, 'I will strike the shepherd, and the sheep of the flock will be scattered.' But after I am raised up, I will go ahead of you to Galilee." (26:30–32)

In these words, Jesus not only furnishes the scenario for what will happen but also completes the training that has been his concern throughout the supper. There is a slight shift in location: the mountain overlooking the Holy City and temple, with all the recent memories. From this mountain can be glimpsed the farther horizons in time and space, along with earth's views of the heavens and the heavens' views of the earth. In this very night is to be telescoped, along with ancient prophecies, the expectations of the immediate future, including the immediate announcement: "You will all become deserters because of me…" This is the setting within which Jesus makes three pointed announcements, for two of which he appeals to an ancient prophet (Zech. 13:7).

"I will strike the shepherd…" Clearly the speaker is God, revealing that what follows is God's own carefully considered choice. God, the Great Shepherd, will strike down this earthly shepherd whom God has sent to redeem God's people Israel. When his hour comes, Jesus makes this will of God his own, thus making his atoning death a joint action with his Father. The striking refers, of course, to the blows inflicted by Jesus' executioners the next day, who both did and did not know what they were doing.

The second announcement follows naturally on the first, both being drawn from Zechariah: "and the sheep…will be scattered." The same God who strikes the shepherd scatters his sheep. These sheep are the twelve shepherds-in-training. Clearly their scattering will be due to their efforts to escape the fate of their Shepherd. Accordingly, this word of God reinforces the earlier word of Jesus. This scattering again represents the convergence of divine and human wills. That it is God who scatters them does not diminish their responsibility, but only accentuates it. The fulfillment of this word from God comes within only an hour or two, for the scattering takes place when Jesus is arrested.

The two predictions simply repeat former warnings that the disciples had received. They lead, however, to a new word, which, coming third, receives the major emphasis. "After I am raised up, I will go ahead of you to Galilee." This makes it clear that the one who strikes the Shepherd will be the one who will raise him. But that is not the point here. Already a new vista opens up that discloses Jesus' (and Matthew's) concern for the period after the resurrection. The humiliation leads to the resurrection, and that makes possible a new trip to Galilee. One part of this Shepherd's mission has been completed; with that meeting the other part will begin. In the first part, the Twelve have filled a special role; in the new part, their role will be even more strategic. Just as God's design will be fulfilled in the humiliation and exaltation of the Shepherd, the same design will be fulfilled in the scattering and reunion of God's sheep. The identification of the crucified blasphemer as Israel's shepherd is an essential part of a single design that now includes the new mountaintop commissioning of the scattered sheep. Readers are told to anticipate that meeting as an essential beginning to everything that will follow.

In these three declarations the story presents the good news in miniature form. The narrator summarizes in these images what has happened to the disciples since their first call and what is about to happen in Jerusalem. He discloses how tightly God has bound the fate of the sheep to that of their shepherd, a fate in which the last will truly become first, because God has given them a role that continues the humiliation and exaltation of their Shepherd.

Episode Five: The Passover Denial

Those three key declarations from the Father and the Son provoke a response from all the disciples, for whom Peter, as usual, speaks: "Even though all the others will be caused to stumble because of you, I will never be one of them." Readers will recall earlier disavowals of this sort. Peter is very facile in self-deception and unwarranted self-confidence. And he shared this confidence and deception with the others. The disciples are not even penitent, for they are as yet unable to know the humiliation that serves as a sign of the kingdom. But they cannot deceive their Shepherd, who tries to penetrate their confidence. "Truly I tell you [the magisterial signature of the Messiah], before the cock crows at the end of this very night, you will deny me three times [proving the truth of God's promise]" (26:34, au. trans.). In these words, the Messiah's knowledge underscores Peter's ignorance, for which, of course he is fully responsible, even though both God and Satan are present as his invisible prompters. His next reply underscores his blindness and deafness. "Even if it should become necessary for me to die with you, I will never deny you" (26:35, au. trans.). In Gospel imagery, the night is defined by such self-deception, such an instinctive claim to be superior to the others, and such unconscious subjection to Satan's power.

It is easy for readers, knowing the later work of Peter, as well as Jesus' earlier approval of the Rock, to discount so bleak and unrelieved a picture of Peter's character. Surely the prince of apostles could not have been so foolish and so weak as this picture suggests. Other readers, however, may take special delight in the demonstration of the stupidity of these so-called heroes of the faith. The story, however, does not encourage either of these reactions.

Rather, the point of the story is this: Even the closest disciples, in their flight at his arrest, prove how impossible to them is the idea of a *crucified* Messiah. By striking the Shepherd, God rejects all human conceptions of messianic deliverance, and with those conceptions all human conceptions of divine power. Peter's denial simply confirms the strength of those conceptions.

Episode Six: The Sheep Are Scattered (26:36–56)

The story of what happened in Gethsemane is so familiar that few comments seem to be needed. Yet some features of the story often escape notice, and these are features that provide important clues to Peter's education. Three disciples are near Jesus in this place of struggle, and as much space is given to them as to Jesus, even though they never respond verbally to his words. The story gives as much attention to their drowsiness as to his agony. His alertness discloses their guilt in sleeping, and their sleeping increases the depth of his aloneness. Three times he comes to them, only to find them asleep, a dramatic acting out of his parable in which the Messiah comes in the middle of the night and surprises his servants (25:1–13). This hour is the time of his greatest suffering. The next afternoon on the cross there is no indication of his physical agony; then one hears only his cry of forsakenness. Because the disciples will not then be present, Gethsemane offers them the only opportunity of sharing in his struggle–and they go to sleep, not once but three times, thus showing the completeness of their indifference. They do not share in his final acceptance of the cup. He recognizes that his hour has come; they do not. Unready for his hour, they are even less ready for their own. In accepting God's will for himself, he uses their sleeping to provide the opportunity to continue their training: "Stay awake and pray that you may not come into the time of trial." (Did the narrator intend here to remind readers of this key petition in their daily prayer?) Even in this hour Jesus cannot forget his own double mission from God: not only to drink his own cup but at the same time to prepare these apostles for their own time of trial. The finality of his own agony gives a mysterious depth and finality to his commands: "Stay awake...watch...pray." The struggle with them is part of his struggle with God. Their failure to watch with him, and his failure in teaching such watchfulness, becomes a component of his own agony. While they are sleeping, Satan sows weeds in the field where, in God's name, Jesus has sown wheat. They are as far as ever from cross-bearing, a fact proved by their headlong flight.

Episode Seven: Peter Saves His Life (26:57–75)

In the story of what happened in the court of Caiaphas, not one but two trials took place. In the trial of Jesus, Caiaphas and the high priests served as judges; in the trial of Peter, the judges were anonymous servant-girls and bystanders. The narrator gave almost as much attention to this second trial as to the first. Both trials represented a conclusion to the earlier stories, one summarizing Jesus' steady faithfulness to vocation, the other, fickle duplicity. The trial of Jesus, in one sense, was no trial at all, since he had already accepted the verdict that fused his own will with that of God. By contrast, the trial of Peter was a genuine trial in which the judges voiced the truth of Peter's identity and his avowed loyalty, while he evaded that truth by lies, his three denials matching Jesus' three rebukes in Gethsemane. Peter remained utterly silent when the judges were searching for reliable witnesses (26:60) but became voluble when he was himself accused–of the truth. The narrator used the two trials to reinforce a double verdict: The honest confession of Jesus threw a spotlight on Peter's dishonest evasions, and these evasions underscored Jesus' honesty. As Jesus' condemnation proved faithfulness to his mission from the beginning, so, too, Peter's denials were consistent with his story from the beginning. Trying to imitate Jesus' victory over the unruly waves, he had first succeeded but then, because of little faith, he had begun to sink. Responding to a revelation from God, he had given his witness that Jesus was the Messiah, but at once he had succumbed to Satan's lies. On the mountain of transfiguration, where he had seen Jesus talking with Moses and Elijah, he had been eager to build three shrines, but had then proved unable to exorcise demons. After Jesus' arrest, he had followed the soldiers to the court to learn what would happen, but had then remained silent among the guards, until he was charged with being a follower of the Galilean impostor. Then he lied before them all and supported his lies with anxious oaths (see 5:33–37). He lost his life by trying to save it. The narrator shows no mercy; that is, until that moment when Peter heard a sound louder than all the accusations: the crowing of the cock.

That natural but penetrating screech transformed the entire situation, even though only one of the actors heard it. For the narrator, that screech introduced another judgment scene in which the education of Simon Peter was completed (his name does not appear again in this Gospel). This later silence about Peter makes it necessary to ask about the echoes of that sound. Many readers are too content with observing the more trivial echoes: the replacement of fear by courage, lies by honesty, and betrayal by remorse. Those effects were obviously present, but much more was at stake.

The voice of the cock reminded Peter of Jesus' words, and in so doing, it became the voice of Jesus. That memory made Jesus fully present to Peter—as the one whom Peter had just denied knowing. Moreover, the voice of the cock announced the transition from night to day, from darkness to light, from blindness to vision, from the dominion of lies to the dominion of truth. In announcing the new day, the cock also announced the day of judgment, God's judgment of the human judges: their kingdom, power, and glory; their interpretation of the scriptures; their charge of blasphemy that concealed their self-interests and self-assurance. The same day of judgment vindicated Jesus, even though it also testified that the charges against him were true: He will destroy the temple and rebuild it in three days; he is "the Messiah, the Son of God." They had judged him a fraudulent Messiah; God claimed him as God's Anointed Son. In vindicating Jesus, however, God had imposed a fearsome verdict on Peter: on his fears and lies, his vulnerability to self-interest and self-deception, his repeated denials, "I do not know the man," which simply proved Jesus' wisdom: "No one knows the Son except the Father" (11:27).

All this was implicit in the tears that the voice of the cock produced. The tears represented Peter's awareness of this day of judgment and his acceptance of God's verdict. The tears spoke of an utter humiliation that proved stronger than his human accusers, stronger even than the Satan-induced denials. In its effects, then, Peter heard again in this morning reveille the first proclamation of his Master: "The kingdom of the heavens is near: repent and believe in the good news." Peter's tears were his response, his repentance, his belief. In his denials he had claimed to be above his teacher. In his tears he realized what it would mean to be "like his teacher," and he accepted that vocation (10:24–25). He confirmed the nearness of God's kingdom.[4]

These changes were indicated in a brief but subtle way by the narrator: "He *went out* and wept bitterly" (26:75). The weeping was preceded by a quiet but dramatic departure. In leaving the trial scene, Peter was declaring both his condemnation of that scene and his own belated freedom from it, both of which he owed to his Master. This *going out* was a dramatic exit that conveyed a final break with the kingdom, power, and glory that Caiaphas' double trial had embodied. This was not the first such dramatic exit in Matthew. When Jesus had first sent the apostles into the harvest field, he had instructed them on how to depart from houses and towns that rejected them. They should shake off the dust of their feet as a judgment even more severe than God's judgment on Sodom and Gomorrah (10:13–15). By leaving the temple, Jesus himself had declared his messianic condemnation (21:17). By leaving Jerusalem, the city that killed the prophets sent to it, he had left Jerusalem a desert (24:1). In a similar way, Peter's departure from the judgment hall dramatized the same divine judgment that was declared by his tears.

Questions for Reflection and Discussion

1. Find three or four hymns in your hymnal that describe the role of disciples at the Last Supper. Does singing those hymns help you understand Matthew? How?

2. With the story and the hymns in mind, share your thoughts on the comment about sin in note 2 (p. 170).

3. How does the Matthean story help to explain the significance of the cock in later art and architecture?

CHAPTER 8

SAVING LIFE BY LOSING IT[1]

*On that day, says the Lord G*OD*,*
    I will make the sun go down at noon,
    and darken the earth in broad daylight.

(Amos 8:9)

The stone that the builders rejected
    has become the chief cornerstone.

(Psalm 118:22)

It may seem strange, in a study of the training of the apostles, to devote a chapter to the account of the death of Jesus, when, as a matter of fact, none of the eleven apostles were present. How can we justify giving so much space to so few verses? When, however, we have regard for the perspective of Matthew himself, such justification is relatively easy, and in this book we are basically concerned with recovering his perspective.

The Outlook of the Narrator

The plan underlying the entire Gospel was designed to reach its goal in the passion story. As Donald Senior has demonstrated, "The Passion story describes the final climactic moment of a fateful choice that has suffused the entire Gospel."[2] Moreover, the longer passion story was written with the account of Jesus' death in mind: "The natural climax of the Passion is the death of Jesus. This, obviously, is the end toward which each scene in the narrative is directed."[3] Without the crucifixion, there would have been no passion story, and without that story, no Gospel. In his first verse Matthew had introduced Jesus as the Messiah; it was the truth and nature of that messiahship that became the decisive point of contention in his crucifixion (1:1; 26:63; 27:17).

The centrality of crucifixion in Matthew's literary plan is demonstrated by the frequent recurrence of five basic motifs and convictions. All five appear together in a brief episode that Matthew placed at a strategic moment, as "Jesus was going up to Jerusalem" for the final time (20:17–29). The first two motifs appear in the clear announcement, "The Son of Man will be handed over to the chief priests and scribes, and they will condemn him to death..." (20:18). This warning continues a theme of messianic suffering that had been intimated in the slaughter of the Bethlehem infants and in the wilderness testing (4:1–11). One of its symbolic expressions is the repeated reference to the cup that the Messiah must drink (20:22; 26:27, 39). The second theme is the assignment to the religious leaders of the responsibility for the Messiah's rejection. Emerging very early during the Galilean ministry, this enmity later became central when Jesus entered Jerusalem and the temple on his last visit. Matthew devoted three long chapters to debates, parables, and woes that explicated the hostility that made the verdict of death inevitable (21–23).

A third motif stressed the requirement that all who followed this Messiah must take up the cross. In the Sermon on the Mount, the concluding beatitude was given to disciples undergoing persecution, while the two concluding antitheses in chapter 5 emphasized the command to love those enemies and to pray for those persecutors. In the first missionary assignment, Jesus stressed the rule that no student could claim a better fate than the teacher, and the announcement that all faithful students would be "hated by all because of my name" (10:22). So it was not strange that, in reply to the ambitious requests of Mrs. Zebedee, Jesus assured her that her sons would also drink his cup. It was to prepare them for such a prospect that Matthew devoted the apocalyptic predictions of chapter 24, the parables of chapter 25, and the discussions in the upper room in chapter 26.[4]

The prospect of suffering for the disciples explains another frequent emphasis in Matthew's story: the uniform inadequacy of their responses. At times, the warning produced total incomprehension: "You do not know..." (20:22). At times they rejected flatly the idea of messianic suffering, with its implication of risk for themselves (16:22). At times, their refusal reflected stubborn blindness, hinted at by the contrast between James and John, on the one hand, and the two blind men of Jericho on the other (20:29ff.). When it finally became certain that their Shepherd would be struck down, they all promised to die with him, though within a few hours all took to their heels at his arrest (26:35, 36).

A fifth motif emerges when we ask what explained Jesus' steadfastness and their cowardice. Martyrdom by itself was not the problem, as hundreds of martyrs for other causes testify. This suffering was unique because it was a result of messianic vocation in obedience to God's law, of which one version was used to introduce the passion story itself: "Whoever wishes to be great among you must be your servant, and whoever wishes to be first among you must be your slave; just as the Son of Man came not to be served but to serve, and to give his life a ransom for many" (20:26–28).

In this compact statement Matthew provided his understanding of God's purpose in the passion: The ransoming of many required that the Messiah become last of all and the slave of all, and his death established the same norm for all disciples. The same norm emerges in many other texts, as, for example, when Jesus distinguished true from false disciples: "All who exalt themselves will be humbled, and all who humble themselves will be exalted" (23:12). Self-humiliation is a common denominator of many edicts of this Messiah: his demand for repentance, for becoming like children, for poverty of spirit and its twin, meekness, for loving enemies, for refusal to judge others and endless forgiveness of them, for becoming last of all, the least and the lowest. In this way Matthew prepared for the passion story by showing how the death of Jesus posed two inescapable issues: Was Jesus' law of self-humiliation indeed the law of God, and, if so, did that clinch the truth of the law "like teacher, like student"? When we consider all that was involved for the apostles in the crucifixion, God's answer to Jesus' question, "Why?" (27:46) became as important for them as for him.

The Outlook of Matthew's Readers

At several strategic places in his scenario Matthew disclosed the conditions that his own readers would be facing by way of the predictions of Jesus himself. For example, after depicting the failures of the Pharisees to fulfill their sacred duties "on Moses' seat," Jesus announced that to them, as sons of Cain, he would send, as sons of Abel, his own prophets, wise men, and scribes (including Peter and the other interns) to continue the work of Jesus himself (23:34–39). The almost certain result would be this: Those guilty of the blood of Abel would flog and pursue and kill those loyal to the crucified Messiah. It could hardly be otherwise. When a messianic claimant had been executed as a blasphemous fraud, what would be done to followers who publicly proclaimed in synagogue and temple that he had indeed been the Son of God, fulfilling through his death the divine law of self-humiliation?

Jesus foresaw not only the dangers to his surrogates in the post-resurrection community; he described in detail some of the results of such dangers within that community. The prospect of criminal prosecution would produce successors to Judas who would betray friends to the authorities. Under pressures of cross-examination, there would be successors to Peter who would deny that they had ever known Jesus. Such betrayals and denials would fan the flames of suspicion and fear among the more loyal; love for the master would cool very quickly (24:7–14). Members of the community wondered how to deal with leaders who were too bold or too cautious; leaders, on their part, needed guidance on how to maintain discipline and unity among fractious followers, new and old. Believers who pooled their resources in response to a common faith found the administration of those resources at a common table a source of great tension. The establishment of common attitudes toward scripture became necessary but increasingly difficult: Which laws remained binding in the new age? What changes should be made in the inherited practices of prayer, fasting, and benevolent giving?

On all such matters Matthew relayed teachings of the Master to guide decisions within each congregation. Especially difficult were the group decisions that would identify Christians as sources of sedition. For example, should they feed, clothe, and offer refuge to believers from a neighboring town who were fleeing the police? And when members were imprisoned and awaiting trial, should others visit them with food and encouragement? Matthew told the story of Gethsemane, in part, as a paradigm of struggles that Jesus' followers would face, and the story of his crucifixion was a paradigm that condensed into one moment all the other issues of this new vocation. In his cry, Jesus quoted from Psalm 22: "My God, my

God, why have you forsaken me?" In their cry, a quotation from the Lamentations of Jeremiah 5:20 would have been apt: "Why have you forgotten *us?*" Answers to that question were not a matter of casual curiosity, but of the lives and deaths of individuals and of congregations. Those who found that their love had grown cold would find in the scripture much to strengthen their doubts and hesitations. The fear of Godforsakenness had been a central theme in the law and the prophets, and texts often seemed to support the adversaries more than the believers. We should look, then, at some key passages.

Forsakenness in Scripture

The Old Testament is full of stories of Israel's forsaking God and of God's responding by forsaking Israel. God had sealed a covenant with Israel that circumscribed its existence from beginning to end. That covenant left no doubt about one law: Whenever Israel would forsake God, God would forsake them (Deut. 28:15–38). For example, when "truth has perished" among his people, God commanded Jeremiah to call out:

Cut off your hair and throw it away;
　　raise a lamentation on the bare heights,
for the LORD has rejected and forsaken
　　the generation that provoked [God's] wrath. (Jer. 7:29)

The same law was as binding on individuals as on the nation: "There is no one to deliver the person whom God has forsaken" (Ps. 71:11, au. trans.). This conviction on the part of both the individual and nation was a silent witness to the centrality of the axis that bound them to their God, as well as the intimacy of that axis. Their world was defined by their awareness of God's presence or absence, their nearness to God or their forsakenness by God. The bond between deity and people was so close as to make this reaction inescapable: "'Because you have forsaken me, I also will forsake you…for you have defiled your hands with blood…It is not as though you had forsaken me; you have forsaken yourselves,' says the Lord" (2 Esd. 1:25–27).[5]

While never downplaying the dire results when Israel forsook its God, other texts stop short of attributing to God an automatic rejection. God's original choice of God's people had not depended on their choice of God; no more did their abandonment of the covenant guarantee God's abandonment of them. So Isaiah countered despair with this reassurance:

> But Zion said, "The LORD has forsaken me,
>   my Lord has forgotten me."
> Can a woman forget her nursing child,
>   or show no compassion for the child of her womb?
> Even these may forget,
>   yet I will not forget you. (Isa. 49:14–15)

Israel preserved two convictions that seemed to contradict each other: God's justice in forsaking Israel and God's mercy in refusing to forsake them. Jeremiah accented the justice:

> I have forsaken my house,
>   I have abandoned my heritage;
> I have given the beloved of my heart
>   into the hands of her enemies. (Jer. 12:7)

Isaiah accented the mercy:

> You [Zion] shall no more be termed Forsaken,
>   and your land shall no more be termed Desolate…
> You shall be called, "Sought Out,
>   A City Not Forsaken." (Isa. 62:4, 12)

The outlook of Jesus and Matthew clearly favored the outlook of Isaiah. On the one hand is the uncompromising judgment on Israel's forsakenness: "O Jerusalem…your house is left to you a desert" (23:37–39, au. trans.). On the other hand, God remains a mother hen calling a wandering brood back under her wings—a call, of course, that God issued by sending Israel messengers in the name of the Lord!

The ambivalence of justice and mercy toward those who forsake God is typical of many biblical writers. There is much less ambivalence, however, about God's response to an Israel that does *not* forsake him. As an expression of this response, the Psalm is quite typical:

> Those who know your name put their trust in you,
>   for you, O LORD, have not forsaken those who seek you.
>   (Ps. 9:10)

So confident was the psalmist of this law that he testified, "I have been young, and now am old, yet I have not seen the righteous forsaken or their children begging bread" (Ps. 37:25). Such confidence was anchored securely in the Mosaic law (Deut. 28:1–14). How deeply this confidence was grounded was reflected in Job's dramatic struggle. As Job's friends insisted, to be forsaken by God was prima facie evidence that Job had forsaken God. The strength of this conviction was illustrated by the very Psalm that Jesus quoted from the cross. The first twenty verses of that Psalm seemed to offer incontestable evidence that a righteous man had indeed been forsaken by the God in whom he had trusted. (The passion story of Jesus carried many echoes of those verses that were resonant with unrelieved dereliction.) But the closing verses of that Psalm corrected all such appearances. Ultimately the forsaken psalmist was rescued by his God "from the wild oxen." Accordingly, after his cry of despair was heard, his protest gave way to praise (22:28). In the end, then, Psalm 22 reinforced the view that God cannot forsake a servant who has been faithful.

If it was difficult to imagine God forsaking a righteous man, it was utterly impossible to imagine God forsaking the Messiah. A Messiah would serve as God's *alter ego* in rescuing God's people from their enemies; a forsaken Messiah would therefore force Israel to reconstruct all expectations concerning God, the Messiah, and what messianic rescue would mean. Before such a reconstruction would become possible, convincing answers to the question *why* would be necessary. So the key question on Golgotha was not, Have you forsaken me? but "*Why* have you...?" That word *why* accepts the actuality of forsakenness and explains the necessity of giving reasons for God's action. If God had not forsaken Jesus, the question would not have arisen. But the question had become pivotal for Matthew's readers, at least some of whom were facing martyrdom. They had responded to the call, "Whoever does not take up the cross...is not worthy of me" (10:38). It was the question *why* for which they needed convincing answers if they were to be prepared for their own tests.

The Forsakenness of Jesus

For various reasons, modern readers may deny that Jesus was forsaken by God, but there can be little doubt that Matthew accented the fact, agreeing with Jesus' adversaries at least on that point. The situation itself provided the most conclusive definition and demonstration of forsakenness. The narrator made all this clear in the careful phrasing of the taunts of the adversaries. Each bit of mockery carried its own disproof of any claim as God's messenger. By their ribald buffoonery of a robe, crown, and scepter, the soldiers proved that his kingship claim was bogus. So, too, the claim to save others was obviously falsified by his inability to save himself. The audacious claim to destroy and to rebuild the temple (a claim that Matthew appears to have accepted) was ridiculous in view of his total helplessness and weakness on the cross. "If you are the Son of God, come down from the cross" (a test that this dying man was unable to pass; 27:40). "If he comes down...we will believe him" (27:42, au. trans.)—that was a promise that the religious leaders knew was quite safe. "He trusts in God"...so if God wants to verify such a ludicrous trust, "let God deliver him now" (27:43). It was by appealing to the fact of forsakenness that all those taunts proved the absurdity of any messianic claim. Rather, they vindicated the charge of blasphemy. Paul cited scripture to show that everyone hanging on a tree was cursed by God; Matthew preferred to indicate the same curse indirectly by citing these self-assured epithets, one after another.

The scene as a whole constituted a visual and audible rejection of Jesus' law that the greatest were those who humbled themselves in order to become the slaves of all; the religious leaders rejected that law in favor of its opposite. On the Golgotha stage, all the actors, except the women, were totally convinced that if God had ever been with this helpless man, God had in the end surely forsaken him. No one present challenged that logic. We may surmise that it was such logic that evoked the terrible cry[6] and that made an answer crucial (in the root sense of that overworked adjective) to Matthew and his readers.

The narrator, however, gave no immediate audible answer to Jesus' cry. Perhaps such an answer would have implied too much temerity, since only God could be trusted with an answer. If, however, we have been justified in looking to Matthew's earlier paragraphs for a definition of forsakenness, we may be justified in looking to the following paragraphs for clues to God's response to the cry *why*. Matthew clearly expected his readers to infer some components of that response from what happened next.

The first component was this: The cynical taunts were followed by a sudden and complete transformation of the stage, scene, and actors. In the midst of the mockery and without warning, the Place of the Skull became the whole earth where at midday three hours of abysmal darkness fell, apparently with an unearthly silence. The crowd, along with its raucous babble, seems to have vanished.

Strangest of all, the eclipse of the sun attracted no notice from the crowd, no excitement, no dread, no wonder. No longer did the thieves, the priests, or the cheering mob take part in the action. Only such human actors remained on the stage as were needed to give awkward verbal responses, first to Jesus' cry and then to the earthquake. Up to this point the story moved steadily forward as though the execution of three criminals on a desolate hill could be understood in ordinary public-eye terms. Beyond this point, however, the stage was shrouded in transcendent mystery in which God was the only actor; the moment had now finally come for God to unveil God's secret purposes. When things happened in the story of which the human actors were unaware (like this darkness), we can be quite sure that here the narrator had his readers in mind. He hoped that with eyes of faith they might be able to see God's work in what had been hidden from the original participants. Up to this point in his narrative, Matthew had taken pains to discourage apocalyptic speculations about the coming of a Messiah, speculations that always seemed to be motivated by the self-interest of the speculators. Now Matthew found that the answers of God to the Messiah were so unexpected as to require the use of apocalyptic language to convey their imponderable scope and depth.

The Cosmic Darkness

The language of apocalypse is fond of the image of darkness, since such darkness was the way in which the struggle in heaven between God and Satan was visualized. Wherever Satan's lies and deceptions succeeded, darkness fell. Because death had from the beginning been the penalty for those deceptions, darkness and death became twin images. Darkness thus became a symbol of God's struggle, not so much with human adversaries as with the rebellious "powers of heaven." There is surely an intended intertextual link between this darkness covering the whole earth at the crucifixion and the earlier prediction of Jesus:

> The sun will be darkened,
>   and the moon will not give its light,
> the stars will fall from heaven,
>   and *the powers of heaven* will be shaken
>   (24:29, emphasis added)

As was typical of apocalyptic imagery, this struggle in heaven was the counterpart of earthly suffering on the part of the faithful:

absolute aloneness and alienation from human help and sympathy, unnerving weakness and debility in the face of massive power, total vulnerability to violence and to the oblivion of the tomb, the apparent futility of work that constituted obedience to God's calling, the victory of enemies through whom Satan has demonstrated power. Such was the darkness that covered the whole earth; it was not limited to one place or to one moment, but surrounded all who had shared, or would share, such forsakenness.

In the same biblical lexicon, this darkness was a sign of God's judgment on the rebellious people, which, in their blindness, they could not see. Such blindness was fully illustrated by the mob that reveled in its blood-guiltiness, by the rulers of the temple, by the interpreters of the law, and even by the other "thieves," all of whom had been deceived by the lies of the serpent, descendants of Cain and residents of "the city that kills the prophets" (23:37). No symbol other than darkness could better connote all these forms of blindness and intransigence.

This was true in part because this darkness was a continuation of that darkness from which the Creator had first separated the light. Matthew wanted his readers to perceive Jesus' crucifixion against the most comprehensive background conceivable. This darkness was a structural feature in human existence that could be removed only by the Creator in line with God's initial design for all things. Only God's powerful Word could wield sufficient authority to create light out of darkness and so heal the people's blindness that they could perceive God's primal purpose and share in its realization. By giving an all-inclusive definition of the self-humiliation of the Messiah, this darkness gave an all-inclusive perception of purposes that were hidden within such forsakenness. Only total darkness could anticipate total light.

The Creation of Light

It is significant that the darkness over the whole earth did not begin with the Messiah's cry, but rather ended with it (27:45). The cry triggered the return of light, a fact that disclosed the narrator's conviction that the light itself provided another component in God's answer to the Messiah's *why*. This light, of course, also reflected the vast expansion of the stage setting. Nothing could be more startling than such a sudden and complete transformation, yet those present on Golgotha showed no awareness of the change from night to day: no surprise, no confusion, no discussion, no explanation. Those who had been so ghoulish in their delight over Jesus' agony, if they were still present, took as little notice of this light as of the darkness; further evidence that the narrator was not reporting what happened with the realism of journalists or historians. He was more intent on linking the self-humiliation of Jesus to the creation of light, a fulfillment of his earlier announcement:

> The people who sat in darkness
>   have seen a great light,
> and for those who sat in the region and shadow of death
>   light has dawned. (4:16)

To describe this cry of the Messiah, Matthew chose the adjective "great" (*megalē*), usually translated "loud" when modifying a sound. This simple adjective had a prominent role in passages reporting apocalyptic visions.[7] Thus, in the vision just cited, to see a *great* light was to see in the surrounding darkness the light of salvation by God. Great voices were those that penetrated the normal barrier between heaven and earth. Jesus' cry in the darkness was great because it articulated a suffering that had not been seen since the world began (24:21) and because it was directed, not to Elijah, but solely to God. In earlier scenes in the Gospel, the same adjective had been used to mark the intersection of heavenly forces with human needs: the storms at sea, the collapse of houses built on sand, the exorcism of demons, the opening of tombs, the trumpet that assembled the saints from every corner of heaven. So too at Golgotha, the power of Jesus' cry did not stem from its decibel volume, but from its immediate access to God, whose response was immediate: the return of light over the whole earth. As the darkness disclosed a final helplessness, so the light disclosed a final victory.[8]

Those effects were introduced by another apocalyptic code word, the prophetic exclamation and command "See" (*idou*). To show the direct link between the death cry and its effects, the NRSV uses the phrase "at that moment" (27:51). That translation has the merit of showing the immediate connection, but it fails to indicate the imperative force of *idou*. In other contexts, the word is translated variously: "look," "see," "take notice," "beware." These exclamations are often used to call attention to God's interventions in human affairs, which are neither expected nor easily recognized. The word appears in this Gospel more than sixty times. Often it prepares readers for the works of God soon to follow or reminds them of what God had spoken through scripture. It marks salient moments when heaven is opened and a voice is heard from above, or when angels or prophets relay messages from God. It punctuates stories of exorcisms and the cures of blindness, deafness, or lameness. Wherever heavenly potencies are released on earth, *idou* warns readers of their presence. Here it was especially appropriate to celebrate the first impact of the light.

The Opened Sanctuary

Look! The curtain of the temple was ripped from top to bottom. (27:51, au. trans.)

The verbs used here and later are in the passive voice, "divine passives," because they pointed to things that only God could do. The accent on *idou* implied that these actions of God required a kind of special seeing; just as the words of God were inaudible, so too, the deeds were invisible, except to prophetic perception of heavenly realities. No one saw the ripping or heard the sound. The priests made no protest; they had in fact left the stage. We can be quite sure that the next day's liturgy was not affected. But the act of destruction was seen as no less real. The narrator had prepared for the act by stressing the mockery, "You who would destroy the temple and build it in three days, save yourself" (27:40). But that mockery stated the truth: By choosing to become last of all, the Messiah had accomplished both the destruction of the temple and the building of a new one. The curtain separated the innermost sanctuary from the public courts. Within the sanctuary was the altar, the mercy seat, where the high priest offered sacrifices for the sins of Israel. The tearing of that curtain ended the need for sacrifice on that altar, thus destroying the need for the temple and its priesthood.

Earlier chapters had prepared readers for such a destruction. This Messiah-elect had expelled the robbers from the temple and had ignored its sanctity by healing the blind and lame there (21:12–16). His cursing of the fig tree had carried a hidden but ominous warning. In parables he had declared that the kingdom of God would be taken away from the priests and elders (21:43). When he cursed the city for killing the prophets, he had declared that its house would be left desolate (23:38); not one stone would remain on another (24:2). When this charge of destroying the temple was raised against him at his trial, it is probable that the narrator accepted the charge as true (26:61).[9] The conclusion is therefore almost certain: The tearing of the curtain constituted the destruction of that temple.

The crucifixion also fulfilled the unwitting prophecy of the mockers that Jesus would rebuild the temple. Jesus had declared earlier that, when the Son of man was present, something greater than the temple was there (12:6). Jesus had spoken about building his church on a rock in such a way that the gates of Hell could not destroy it. In the Last Supper he had created a covenant in his blood, poured out for the sins of many (26:28). So when the location of the temple is determined not by buildings but by the presence of God and the effective forgiveness of sins, the creation of a new temple in his death is one of God's answers to the question *why*.

In one of his parables addressed to his enemies, Jesus had told of a landowner who had leased his vineyard to tenants who, instead of giving him his share of the harvest, had murdered his son. He had then asked the chief priests and elders what the landowner would do. They had replied, "He will put those wretches to a miserable death, and lease the vineyard to other tenants who will give him the produce at the harvest time" (21:41). Such was the situation when, with the return of light, the curtain to the sanctuary was torn from top to bottom. Paul said much the same thing when he wrote that in Christ Jesus, God had established "a place of atonement by his blood, effective through faith" (Rom. 3:25, au. trans.). And we read of the same destruction and rebuilding in the epistle to the Hebrews: Jesus "entered once for all into the Holy Place, not with the blood of goats and calves, but with his own blood, thus obtaining eternal redemption" (Heb. 9:12). Thus, on hearing or reading of the torn curtain in the sanctuary, Matthew's readers would also gain "confidence to enter the sanctuary by the blood of Jesus" (Heb. 10:19).[10]

The Opened Tombs

In the same sentence that described the split curtain, the narrator described the splitting of the rocks, and the same verb was used.

> ...and the earth was shaken, and the rocks were split, and the tombs were opened, and many bodies of the holy ones who had fallen asleep were raised, and having come out of the tombs after his resurrection they entered the holy city and appeared to many. (27:51–53, au. trans.)

The story proceeds on the expanded stage, since these tombs were located in various places, and these saints had fallen asleep at different times. But with the return of light, the authority of the earth to imprison them was broken and their *holiness* entitled them to enter the *holy* city. By the forsakenness of Jesus, their own forsakenness was ended.

In his earlier chapters, Matthew had also prepared for this feature in his story. Those very tombs had indeed figured prominently in Jesus' attack on the scribes and Pharisees immediately before his announcement of Jerusalem's desolation and his own final exit from the temple (23:29–24:1). There are many links between that earlier scene and Golgotha: the predictions of persecution and crucifixions, the reference to the blood shed on the earth, the guilt for that blood, the building and decoration of the tombs of the prophets, the desolation of the temple. In both stories, the narrator used the exclamatory command *idou* to call for the special vision needed to recognize what had happened.[11] In both scenes the adversaries were the same: the descendants of two prototypes, the first human brothers, Cain and Abel. Cain is the prototype of those who build and decorate memorials to the former saints; together they form a single generation whose origin Jesus traced even before Cain to the serpent of Eden. It was as "children of vipers" that Jesus had ordered them to "fill up the measure of your fathers," a command that they obeyed on Golgotha. By implication, Jesus and his disciples represented the descendants of Abel, a generation of those bonded by the vicarious shedding of their own blood. So in chapter 23 the narrator had carefully prepared for the later story of the splitting of the rocks.

As the victory of light over darkness required a shaking of the heavens to displace the evil powers, so the freeing of the entombed saints required a shaking of the earth. By splitting the rocks, God declared the condemnation of the Cain generation and the vindication of the Abel. Those who mocked the crucified Messiah because of his helplessness were now mocked by God in opening the very tombs that those mockers had used to prove their own holiness.[12] It is possible also that Matthew saw in the Golgotha quake a fulfillment of Ezekiel's prophecy: "Thus says the Lord GOD: 'I am going to open your graves, and bring you up from your graves, O my people...And you shall know that I am the LORD...I will put my spirit within you, and you shall live'" (Ezek. 37:12–14).

In his account of Jesus' death, Matthew told not only of old tombs opened but of a new tomb that was closed. A rich disciple named Joseph used his own new tomb for Jesus; it was carved out of solid rock, and, after Jesus' body was laid inside, its security was assured by a great stone rolled to block any access. Joseph seems to have been unaware of the earthquake that had opened the other tombs. Why did this narrator juxtapose the two episodes? Did he want to show that, in being buried, Jesus had shared the imprisonment of those earlier prophets? Or did he want to deplore Joseph's blindness to the fact that those earlier tombs had already been opened? Recalling the irony in Jesus' picture of the Pharisees building and reverencing the prophets' tombs (23:29ff.), it is possible that Matthew wanted to show the kinship between this rich disciple and those hypocrites. This narrator was not very kind to the disciples! He was, to be sure, even less kind to the soldiers who were assigned the futile task of guarding the tomb of Jesus *after* his atoning death had had its greatest effects (27:62–66).

The epistle to the Hebrews provides an instructive analogy to the Matthean account of the holy ones entering the holy city (12:22ff.). We find there a highly developed contrast between the two mountains and the two cities. Among the residents of the "heavenly Jerusalem, the city of the living God" are "the spirits of the righteous who have been made perfect." These saints have shared the faith of Abel and of all those praised in chapter 11, all of whom have been made perfect through Jesus' endurance of the cross (12:1–2). Christians who are sprinkled with the blood of Jesus enter that city and share its life with those saints. This epistle believed with the Gospel that the new covenant in Jesus' blood had demonstrated its power to open tombs.[13]

In short, then, the Matthean storyteller included four actions of God as components in God's answer to the Golgotha cry of God's Son: Why? God spoke through the descent of darkness over the whole earth, through the restoration of light, through the splitting of the temple curtain, and through the opening of the saints' tombs. These four actions signified the gift to the Messiah of all authority over heaven and earth, though none of the actors on Golgotha could be aware of that gift. It may be, however, that a fifth episode marked an exception.

The Centurion's Confession

Now when the centurion and those with him, who were keeping watch over Jesus, saw the earthquake and what had taken place, they were so terrified that they said, "Truly, this was God's Son." (27:54, au. trans.)

How did the narrator expect his readers to understand this terror and this confession? These men represented the civil government, with authority extending through Pilate to the emperor. This was the authority that had ordered the execution and would order similar penalties on Matthew's readers. These were the men who had scourged Jesus and whose scoffing had reached its ultimate blasphemy in the graffiti over the cross, "The King of the Jews." These were the men of power who were now terrified by what had transpired. How was such terror to be understood?

Readers could recall a similar instance of terror at the outset of the Gospel. When the wise men from the East, led by the star, had inquired in Jerusalem where the king of the Jews was to be born, King Herod had been frightened "and all Jerusalem with him" (2:3). So great was the terror that Herod ordered the murder of all the children in or near Bethlehem, though his efforts proved futile. Similar efforts at the end of the Gospel proved futile as well. Elsewhere in the Gospel the unexpected display of heavenly power and of human futility had evoked terror. Readers could recall the storms at sea when the disciples' fears had been described in sharpest contrast to Jesus' confidence. There was also their reaction at the transfiguration, when they saw Moses and Elijah talking with Jesus (17:6–7). Such terror was the normal human reaction to the epiphany of a kind of power that left people aware of their own impotence (see 28:4). In the case of Roman power, Jesus had earlier made that contrast clear: "The rulers of the Gentiles lord it over them, and their great ones are tyrants over them. It will not be so among you..." (20:25–26). Of that contrast, the terror of the soldiers at Golgotha was a reminder.

Both the contrast and the terror found expression in the centurion's words: "God's Son." Earlier the soldiers had used the scornful title "The King of the Jews," a title that implied the same kind of king and kingdom as that of Rome. The new title recognized a different kind of power, conferred not by human authority but by divine authority. Coming from a Gentile, this confession was further evidence of the tearing of the temple curtain, inasmuch as Gentiles had not been allowed to go through that curtain into the Holy of Holies (see 12:21). It was evidence also of the earthquake that released saints from their tombs, something well beyond imperial competence. Readers could recall another centurion whose faith Jesus had found superior to anything in Israel (8:5–12). This incident, however, was even more startling. A representative of the highest earthly authority recognized in the man whom he had just executed one to whom God had given supreme authority! But his terror and confession seem to have taken place on an empty stage. An amazing reversal of roles, yet no one else was reported as being amazed. An incredible confession, yet there was no one to cast doubt. To whom, then, did the centurion confess? Did anyone hear? If so, when and where? We know only of the narrator and his readers who would accept the story as another answer by God to Jesus' cry.[14]

A Silent Witness

The narrator took special interest in observing the presence at Golgotha of another person, a silent witness to what happened. The women who had come from Galilee with Jesus were standing "far off." Among them was one whom Matthew alone of the evangelists mentioned: the mother of the sons of Zebedee, James and John, who were, with Peter, Jesus' closest disciples. In the New Testament she is mentioned only twice in incidents that were closely connected. The first of these occasions had come just as Jesus was "on the way," going up to Jerusalem to be crucified. Indeed, the woman, whom we call Mrs. Zebedee, posed a request for Jesus immediately after he had predicted the coming crucifixion. At that strategic moment she made this request: "Declare that these two sons of mine will sit, one at your right hand and one at your left, in your kingdom" (20:21). Jesus' responses were such as to anticipate the later scene.

First of all, he told Mrs. Zebedee that she did not know what she was asking. She did not know the character of his kingdom or how he would qualify for authority within it. He would enter it only by drinking the cup, the cup that he would mention at the Last Supper and in Gethsemane. When he questioned her sons, it became clear that neither they nor their mother understood what he was talking about. (The two sons, of course, though privileged to be present in Gethsemane, were among those who fled at his arrest.) Mrs. Zebedee assumed that in his kingdom places of power would be awarded in ways similar to earthly kingdoms. Jesus replied by distinguishing God's kingdom from "the rulers of the Gentiles." Golgotha demonstrated that distinction. Mrs. Zebedee assumed that first places conferred power; Golgotha proved that in God's kingdom the first place belonged to the powerless slave who "gave his life a ransom for many." So at the Place of the Skull, when she saw Jesus enthroned on a cross, this mother saw two others enthroned, one on the right hand and one on the left, but they were thieves! By taking special notice of the mother's presence at the crucifixion, the narrator invited readers to detect the multiple resonances between the two occasions, the first when Jesus predicted the cross and the second when he hung on it. The presence of Mrs. Zebedee and her two companions provided essential narrative links, first to the earlier predictions of his death and then to remind his apostles of his earlier pledge to go ahead of them to Galilee. The absence of the apostles from Golgotha in no way diminished the narrator's concern for the education of Peter and the others. In fact, Jesus' first sentence to them after their reunion in Galilee was a summary of God's answer to Jesus' cry, *Why?*

Questions for Reflection and Discussion

1. Study the hymns in your hymnal that deal with the crucifixion of Jesus. Which of these seems to you to be closest in spirit to Matthew's account?

2. Does Matthew's account of the passion story support the Moltmann statement in note 10? The Rupp statement in note 11? If not, why not? If yes, how important do they become?

3. When you next gather for worship, it will probably be in a space where the cross or crucifix is the central symbol. How does the study of Matthew contribute to your worship "beneath" that cross?

CHAPTER 9

SHEEP BECOMING SHEPHERDS

[The angel:] There you will see him...
[Jesus:] There they will see me...
[Matthew:] When they saw him...
[Jesus:] See! I will be with you...

(Matthew 28:7, 10, 17, 20, au. trans.)

[Jesus:] Blessed are your eyes, for they see...

(Matthew 13:16)

To imagine the real is to see things that, because of their heavenly provenance, are hidden from normal sight. Thus, at the outset, astrologers from the East (and no one else) had reported, "We have seen his star," and many Galileans sitting in darkness had seen a great light. Jesus traced the blindness of the Pharisees to their inability to perceive the sign of God's kingdom. On many occasions Jesus had rebuked his interns for similar blindness. It is not surprising, then, that the account of their final meeting with their glorified Lord should first promise, then announce, and then declare such a vision. We turn, then, to that account as providing the final stage in the apostles' training (28:16–20).

Few Christians can read Matthew's version of that meeting without unconsciously recalling their memories of the other gospels and without filtering their reactions through centuries of church tradition and doctrine. Nowhere is this conditioning more intrusive than in reading this account of the resurrection. In my analysis I will try to avoid such distortions by treating this story in Matthew solely in the light of his intentions as clarified by clues and anticipations provided by earlier stories. Rereading the story in this fashion, I will view it as designed not so much as a basis for human faith in Jesus' resurrection, but as a set of instructions marking the conclusion of his meetings with the disciples, the inception of their later work, and thereby the conclusion of Jesus' own assignment.

The narrator prepared the way for these instructions by his account of the meeting between an angel and the two women, and then by their meeting with Jesus himself. The presence of *two* women fulfilled the biblical requirement for two witnesses to validate strategic events. The women experience strong emotions–fear, joy, adoration– but these are immediately replaced by the task entrusted to them. Their two meetings, first with the angel and then with Jesus, give primary weight to directions designed for the disciples. Jesus' instructions virtually repeat those of the angel: "Go and tell my brothers to go to Galilee; there they will see me" (28:10).

The words suggest three inferences. The primary accent falls on the command *Go.* The reference to his resurrection is replaced by the assurance that the disciples would *see him* in Galilee on the mountain. Presumably, seeing him will assure them of his heavenly authority, its reality and dependability. Now he speaks of them as his brothers, implying a new bond between heaven and earth, established simultaneously with him and their Father.

The narrator seems to have chosen the words with great care as a preparation for the mountain rendezvous. On that occasion, a similar care was shown: "When they saw him, they worshiped him; but some doubted. And Jesus came and said to them…" (28:17–18).

Their seeing fulfilled his promise, both to the women and earlier to the disciples (26:32). Their spontaneous reactions of worship and doubt suggest that they saw him in heaven, exalted to a role in which both reactions were to be expected. This suggestion is supported by the next verse: He *came to* them; that is, the vision preceded the coming. He came from his exalted throne, from heaven to earth, where he could give his directions to them in the language of earth and promise them his continued presence with them in their work.

Jesus and the Eleven

The focus on the disciples is clear, for they and no others are present with Jesus. There is an inevitable change in the number because of Judas' betrayal and suicide. This occasion completes a process of education that had begun with the summons of the four fishermen and the first lecture on the Galilean mountain. Jesus' new status fulfilled promises repeatedly made to these students and to them alone. In doing so, it quietly corrected their earlier blindness and reversed earlier rejections of those promises. The narrator accomplishes this with great economy of words: He announces what has happened in heaven, mandates their new duties, and issues a new promise covering their future bonds (28:18–20). The final promise leaves nothing more to be said about either teacher or students. The narrator has fulfilled his objectives, even though these parting words of Jesus' invite readers to imagine how in fact these students would later fulfill their newly assigned roles as teachers.

> The disciples went to Galilee, to the mountain where Jesus appointed them...(28:16, au. trans.)

On leaving the room where they had eaten together and on reaching the mountain of Olives, Jesus had told them, "After I am raised up, I will go ahead of you to Galilee" (26:32). The meeting and its location are specific. Later, on Easter morning, the instructions are also specific: The mountain in Galilee is mentioned not once but twice. Now, in order to specify the location even more exactly, the narrator adds one further detail: It is the mountain where Jesus had *appointed* them. That detail was designed to help readers identify the actual mountain, but it does this only if we return to the traditional translation of this verse.

Until our own century, major English versions translated the Greek verb *tasso* into the English "appointed."[1] Beginning with the Revised Standard Version, however, translators have preferred another translation of the Greek verb and have followed the suggestion of the standard Greek lexicon: "the mountain to which Jesus directed them." These later translations are based on the assumption that Matthew had nowhere mentioned their *appointment* on a mountain; they assume, rather, that Matthew was referring to 26:32, even though that verse had not specified a particular mountain. In chapter 2 I presented evidence for an *appointment* of the disciples on the first Galilean mountain: "You are the salt of the earth." I therefore prefer the basic definition of the Greek verb: "to appoint or establish in an office" or "to put someone in charge over someone." I believe, therefore, that the instruction in chapter 28 referred to the mountain where Jesus had begun his training of disciples for later leadership in the crowds of followers. Accordingly, I believe that for this final sermon the narrator intended to return full circle to the strategic beginning of their training, in this way reinforcing those first directions as applicable now to the period following Jesus' death. Simultaneously, the narrator gave a more ultimate "heavenly" authority to all earlier instructions–in chapters 10, 18, and 23–25. In short, the location of this mountain was specified for important reasons.

> When they saw him, they worshiped him; but some doubted... (28:17)

Their earlier blindness was now corrected. This *seeing* represented the fulfillment of many earlier predictions. It is a human seeing from an earthly position, but it is a vision of heavenly truth, a temporal vision of the eternally real. The angel and the risen Lord have penetrated the screen separating heaven from earth, and the double reaction was typical of such epiphanies: worship and doubt. Theophanies and christophanies give space to both reactions; although the vision is real, its reality is always subject to doubt. In this case, both reactions are almost immediately replaced by the words spoken, vision giving way to audition, human awe and wonder giving way to quite intelligible heavenly directions. Readers should note that the narrator does not pause to support the authenticity of the vision, to identify the person seen, or to answer questions raised by doubting readers. He assumes the reality of the conversation of teacher-with-students and turns immediately to its substance.

This turning from seeing to hearing is characteristic of the entire Gospel. Recall, for example, the transition in the story of Caesarea Philippi from God's revelation of Jesus as the Messiah to the translation in words of that revelation, or the account of the transfiguration vision that ended in decisive words. Human visions of heavenly presences are incomplete for this narrator apart from human audition of heavenly imperatives. The account of the vision of the exalted Messiah passed immediately from the seeing to the hearing, from reactions of human worship and doubt to earthly students' listening to orders from their clearly identified heavenly teacher.

New Authority

At the outset Jesus clarifies the change in his status: "All authority in heaven and on earth has been given to me..." (28:18). The identity of the giver is unmistakable: the God who has now conferred this new status. As creator and judge of all things, he alone is qualified to make such a gift. (Satan's offer of a similar status [4:1–11] had been deceptive and spurious.) God has now made the gift without stipulations or conditions: "All." This statement accents a newly confirmed authority "in heaven," because in his baptism Jesus had received authority on earth, which crowds had recognized from the beginning (7:29). It had also been recognized by demons and by a Roman centurion. The Son of man had exercised authority on earth to forgive sins. Jesus had even shared that authority with his apostles-designate in their first journeys as newscasters. Acting under that authority, Jesus had completed his mission on earth as a prophet, healer, and teacher.

Now his authority had been enlarged to include heaven, the source of all authority.[2] His sonship and Messiahship had been confirmed in the highest quarters. In and through him, the kingdom had come near to earth; he had defeated the powers of Satan, first after his baptism and now in his death. In and through him, darkness had fallen over the whole earth and a new day had dawned. First sent to Israel, he had assigned these interns to Israel; now exalted to heaven, with authority over all nations, he sends them to all nations. The command center for his work through the Eleven has shifted from earth to heaven, and with that shift the work has gained final authority. In this extended conversation (28:18–20), one verb appears in the imperative mode, while three appear as participles, although they, too, carry imperatival force: go, make disciples, baptize, teach. Perhaps the greatest weight falls upon the command to make disciples.

Go! The meaning seems to be obvious. Now, however, unlike the earlier commands issued on earth (e.g., 5:13; 10:1–4), the command issues from heaven. With this origin, the command carries an indefinable height and depth. According to the narrator's thought-world, when the disciples go, they will move from heaven to earth and not simply from Galilee to other regions of earth. Those who receive or reject them will receive or reject God's intervention from heaven. (A mountain, we recall, provides a natural transit point for commerce between heaven and earth.)

Make disciples of all nations. Their going is for this purpose and this purpose only. The other two commands spell out what is included within this command. Interpreters have found this command ambiguous at two points.

First, the word translated as "nations" (ethnē) can as readily be translated "Gentiles." Some contextual considerations favor the latter choice. The location of the mountain is carefully specified as Galilee, a region with a large Gentile population, which was therefore scorned by many Jews. It was far removed from the Holy City and the temple that God had specially blessed. In fact, the region was often dubbed "Galilee of the Gentiles." To be a Galilean was cause for scorn and suspicion (26:69). For the Messiah, on being exalted to heaven, to direct the Eleven to make disciples of all Gentiles would represent a significant divine choice, for their earlier assignment had been limited to "the lost sheep of the house of Israel" (10:6). The Messiah's increased authority and the wider assignment of his disciples constituted a negative verdict on the earthly Jerusalem, expressing a divine judgment on Israel's crucifixion of its own Messiah (see 23:37–38). To adopt the translation "Gentiles," however, would imply a decision against any further mission to Israel, contradicting the underlying thrust of the earlier chapters. So far as we know, none of the early apostles opposed continued work within Israel. The translation "nations" includes Israel; thus, it should be preferred.

The second ambiguity involves the precise meaning of the command to "make disciples." The verb is used only three times in Matthew (13:52; 27:57; 28:19), so interpreters must rely on the context in choosing between two major options. Ordinarily readers suppose that to make disciples is simply to convert unbelievers into believers by persuading them to accept Jesus as Lord and Savior. Missionaries go out to make such converts and, if successful, they call them disciples.[3] People rarely consider the alternative option, one that is, I think, more at home in this Gospel. In chapter 2 I have argued that, with few if any exceptions, this narrator limits the term *disciple* to those carefully selected believers whom Jesus authorized as messengers to proclaim the good news of the kingdom and to teach and judge the "crowds" of believers. Disciples are those who had left homes, occupations, families, and fixed residences, and had become prophetic mendicants moving from house to house and village to village. Should we adopt that picture of their vocation as a basis for understanding the meaning of *making* disciples, we would conclude that Jesus is here employing his new heavenly authority to give them a new task. As his representatives on earth, they are now to do what he has been doing with them: With their new authority they must begin to select and train successors to carry on their essential roles. As the first contingent of disciples had been drawn from Israel and sent to Israel, this new contingent must be drawn from all nations (or Gentiles) and sent to all nations (or Gentiles). I submit that the following two commands support this understanding of Jesus' command: "Make disciples of all nations."

The Baptism

The third command is, "Baptize them into the name of the Father and of the Son and of the Holy Spirit" (28:19, au. trans.). If there is to be only a limited number of those commissioned to continue Jesus' mission to all nations, how is this first contingent of disciples to *make* new disciples? The most obvious answer is the best: They must confer on these new messengers authority from the highest source to carry out their specialized vocation. It is the bestowal of such authority that is the object of this third command. New apostles must receive this triple heavenly authority (authority is the primary force of the metaphor "the name"). Baptism conveys that authority.

It is difficult, however, for most readers to link baptism to this conferring of apostolic authority. This difficulty stems from the subsequent use of *baptism* to refer to the admission of believers into membership within the church. If Matthew's use of the term was different from this general use, most readers will demand a careful review of the evidence. This calls for an examination of every appearance of the term *baptism* in this Gospel.

According to Matthew's story, Jesus did not baptize anyone, or if he did, this narrator makes no mention of it. He did not baptize the twelve disciples whom he so thoroughly trained. And when he sent them through the towns of Israel with his message of the kingdom, he did not suggest that they should baptize those who welcomed them and to whom they gave God's peace. In none of his teachings did Jesus command believers to register their humility by being baptized. He both taught and commanded that all treasures should be invested in heaven, but nowhere linked such investment to baptism. He invited the weary and burdened to come to him, but that invitation allowed no place for a ritualistic act. With this background, then, it would be very surprising if at the end he should command the Eleven, who had not been baptized, to baptize *all* who believed in the good news. How can we explain such a command at this point? How can this command be explained in Matthew's terms?

One clue to an answer may be found in Matthew's description of the baptism of Jesus himself. He had defined his own baptism as repentance, defining repentance as the fulfillment of all righteousness. In his opening lecture, Jesus gave a triple expansion of this definition. In the case of the crowds, whom he had healed by liberating them from multiple kinds of bondage without baptism, Jesus defined repentance by means of the eight beatitudes. In the case of the disciples, he had defined repentance positively by their work as the salt and the light and negatively by the righteousness of the scribes and Pharisees. In the case of Jesus himself, his own fulfillment of all righteousness was declared to be a fulfillment of the law and the prophets. The account of Jesus' baptism by John itself includes a very clear declaration of the meaning of that baptism. The descent of the Spirit and the voice from heaven together reveal the descent of heavenly authority on to God's Son. It is that gift of authority that Satan immediately tests, without success. That same gift qualifies Jesus to announce the nearness of the kingdom of the heavens. Thus, Matthew's account of Jesus' baptism defines that baptism in terms of a transfer of authority from heaven to earth. John himself announces that Jesus will baptize "with the Holy Spirit and fire" (3:11). So in this entire Gospel there are only two references to baptism in connection with the mission of Jesus or his apostles; one comes at the inauguration of Jesus' authority and the other when he authorizes his apostles to baptize others.

All other references to baptism speak of John the Baptist. He is the one known as "the Baptist," not Jesus and not Jesus' apostles. Only once does Jesus speak of the meaning of John's baptism, and there he indirectly defines its significance: "Did the baptism of John come from heaven, or was it of human origin?" (21:25).

Jesus posed this question as an answer to the chief priests and elders who were questioning Jesus' authority. When they refused to answer the question about John's authority, Jesus also refused: "Neither will I tell you by what authority I am doing these things" (21:27). Jesus' question about John and his answer about himself combine to make clear what Jesus meant by baptism. It is *the exercise of authority received from heaven.* John had received such authority; in his final commission to his prophets, Jesus authorized his successors to exercise that authority.

This outlook is further clarified by the careful choice of prepositions in Jesus' command: "baptize *into* the name of..." The

Greek preposition is *eis* ("into") not *en* ("in"); the basic use of *eis* with an accusative noun is to represent movement into or toward a place, a goal, or a state of being. To be sure, in ancient practice the two prepositions had become almost interchangeable, but this is not true of Matthew, who referred to John's baptism with *en* but to Jesus' baptism with *eis*. In this case, Matthew is not adding a ceremonial duty to the other duties of the apostles, but is speaking of introducing new recruits into work that is empowered by the authority and grace of the Father, the Son, and the Holy Spirit. At the very time they are first given new power to *make disciples,* they receive authority to share their own heavenly authority with those new recruits. No visible rite was necessary to mark this transition. What was essential was maintaining the succession of authorized fishermen, shepherds, and harvesters. Just as Jesus' own baptism marked his induction into his heavenly authorized vocation, so, too, this baptism—the only one ever ordered by Jesus, according to Matthew—marked the induction of a new generation of apostles into their quite unique vocation. Just as Paul had used the figure of baptism to refer to sharing in the life-giving, life-saving death of Jesus (Rom. 6:1–11), so Matthew used that figure to refer to induction into the triune authority that the exalted Jesus shared with the Eleven.

At this point we should recall the precise form of the prediction made by the prophet John when he baptized Jesus. John did not anticipate another baptism in water. In fact, in his prediction he drew a sharp contrast between his baptism and Jesus': "I baptize you in water into repentance. But coming after me is one more powerful than I am…He will baptize you in the Holy Spirit and fire" (3:11, au. trans.).

The contrast is explicit. In fact, two features are contrasted. Jesus as successor prophet will have greater power and authority. He will also baptize in a different element, not in water but in the Holy Spirit and fire. It is that prediction, with its double contrast, that is fulfilled on the Galilean mountain. There Jesus baptized his successors with the Holy Spirit and fire, and he commanded them to extend that same baptism to their successors.

What is essential to the story, then, is not a new sacrament, but the transfer of authority. Such a transfer is indicated by the phrase "into the name of." The earlier work of the disciples had been done *only* in the name of the prophet Jesus, who came announcing the approach of the kingdom of the heavens. Then they had been speaking for him and acting as his representatives (10:40–42). With his exaltation to heaven, there has now come an extension of authority, first for the Eleven and then for their successors. In the baptism of Jesus as Son, both the Father and the Spirit have been active (3:16, 17); now all three–the Father, the Son, and the Spirit– furnish the heavenly base from which disciples, old and new, receive authority to carry out their mission on earth (compare 1 Cor. 1:13– 17). Matthew could conceive of no better place for this transfer of authority than the Galilean mountain where Jesus had first commissioned the salt of the earth, the light of the world. To use a more modern figure than baptism, we might now visualize this event as graduation exercises in which an authority is conferred; and, with the authority, a charge to the candidates–a charge in which onetime students receive authorization to become teachers.

The Teaching

Because the command to teach seems relatively easy to understand, it is all too easy to misconstrue its original significance. The teacher is obviously the onetime prophet to whom all authority in heaven has now been extended. The students are the eleven disciples, who had previously been given a more limited authority for their work on earth and who had only recently denied and betrayed him. Women had summoned them to this mountain where they had first "matriculated." Here their teacher, with a vastly extended authority, has widened the range of their work and given them enhanced authority for accomplishing his goal. There is no suggestion of canceling their former task of proclaiming the good news, healing the sick, and expelling demons (10:5–15); but two tasks have been added. They are to make disciples, including Gentiles as well as Jews, who will receive authority from the Father, the Son, and the Holy Spirit, and they are to teach those successors to obey all the commands that Jesus has given them. For the first time the students now become teachers, and the master teacher defines the curriculum that they are to use: his own teachings as found in chapters 5–7, 10, 18, and 23–25. His words have now received an enhanced authority because they are now issued in the triune name. There could be no higher imprimatur.

Rereading those earlier teachings in the light of this new imprimatur, it becomes clear that they are well designed for the special tasks of messengers whose authority comes not from earth but from heaven. By leaving homes, occupations, securities, and exalted status on earth, they have surrendered any earth-based standing and therefore can announce the news of the heavenly kingdom without the slightest conflict of interest. Opposition and persecution are inevitable, and many commands are designed to prepare them for that contingency. Going from house to house with no supply of food, they must not be anxious. Although they are as powerless as birds that fly today and fall tomorrow, they must trust the heavenly Father to feed them, knowing that no bird falls to the ground without that Father. Inclined to resent and resist hostility of all kinds, they are ordered to reckon anger as an act of murder, to return good for evil, to love the enemy, and to pray for their persecutors. Summoned before councils and judges, they must reject any temptation to hedge their confession; their yes must mean *yes,* their no, *no;* the slightest effort to deceive inquisitors comes from Satan alone. They cannot obey both God and Caesar, God and Mammon. They cannot store up treasures both on earth and in heaven. Their righteousness must exceed that of the scribes and Pharisees, and, like their Master, they must seek first God's own righteousness. That divine righteousness, as manifested in God's Son, requires that they, too, humble themselves as last of all, slaves to all. That must remain their goal. Suffering itself is not the goal; rather, the passion of Jesus and of his authorized representatives is seen as an inevitable result of rejecting and reversing earthly standards of greatness, of glory, of power, of righteousness.

The disciples are responsible for teaching God's standards, and thus for demonstrating on earth the heavenly vindication of those standards in place of the deceptive standards of Satan (always eager to turn disciples into false prophets [7:15]). It is their active participation in this heavenly conflict between God's kingdom and Satan's that gives force to the concluding petitions in the prayer: "Do not lead us into the time of testing, but rescue us from the Evil One" (6:13, au. trans.). This extensive body of Jesus' commands now provides the essential definition of his final mandate to the Eleven, which they in turn would relay to their successors.

As a reinforcement of this understanding of Jesus' commission, readers should observe that the demands Jesus had issued for the crowds of followers had been of a different type. The demands that had accompanied his announcement of God's kingdom had simply been to repent and to believe in such news. Their repentance was much more than a momentary act of remorse or regret for sins. It was a poverty of spirit well defined by such beatitudes as meekness, mercy, purity of heart, hunger for righteousness. The antithesis of repentance was illustrated by the evasive and defensive self-righteousness of synagogue leaders who, unlike Nineveh, refused such humility. Jesus' call was an invitation from a position *below* that of the blind and demon-possessed, the prostitutes and traitors. Those who found no offense in Jesus' position of lowliness were blessed (11:6), for that lowliness was the *incognito* of a Messiah whom the earth could only see as an anti-Messiah. Only as the humblest slave of all could the heavenly Messiah both draw to himself the humble and offend the exalted. So now the ones whom the Eleven would "make disciples" must also qualify for their work by obeying all the commands that were epitomized in the oxymoron: the exalted will be humbled and the humble will be exalted. In this way the final mandate of Jesus opened the same oxymoronic vista that all his previous demands had reflected (see chapter 6).

So complete was Matthew's interest in these four imperatives (28:18–20) that he made no mention of matters that many readers wish to know. What the narrator omitted is itself significant. He makes no effort to convince anyone, whether original participants or later readers, of the reality of the risen Lord. He does not try to describe the kind of body given to this Messiah by God. He shows no interest in describing what had happened to the Eleven between their panic-stricken flight and their return to this mountain. What had happened to their fears and doubts? Had these messengers been subject, like Peter, to weeping bitterly over their own duplicity? Had the Golgotha earthquake shaken them loose from their preoccupation with their own survival? We do not learn any of this from Matthew. In Matthew's story of this final moment, Jesus does not mention their behavior, does not try to capitalize on their cowardice or offer any sign of forgiveness. Nor does he use his new throne for issuing further denunciations of the earthly authorities in the synagogue or temple. No. The omission of such matters enables Jesus (and Matthew) to concentrate attention on the essentials: a new work that has become possible with Jesus' gift of "all authority." Now he could send the Eleven into their work as teachers and command them to make disciples who would continue that work.

These four imperatives illustrate a characteristic of Matthew's thought-world to which we called attention at the outset, that is, his fusion of three perspectives: the vocation of Jesus, the vocation of Matthew, and the adoption of the heavens as a baseline[4] from which to comprehend God's design for earth. When we consider the four imperatives, this fusion becomes apparent. The commands are issued with the full authority of heaven to articulate God's design for all time and all space. They reiterate and reinforce the vocation of Jesus as teacher, shepherd, Messiah. Simultaneously they define the vocation of the Eleven and their successors, a vocation now to be directed to all nations, calling for repentance and faith from all earth's inhabitants.

Those capable of imagining the force of these commands should be able to comprehend the promise with which Jesus completes his task. This promise begins with a sudden and almost explosive exclamation: "See! Look! Listen!" What follows is a promise both to be seen (as a climax to the chain of *seeings*) and to be heard (this is my bond with you in a common work). "I am with you every day from now on to the consummation of the age…" This is the voice of heavenly authority, the voice of one who demands of his delegates on earth that they, too, carry the cross. He is speaking to disciples who until then had refused that task. But for those who obey, it is the promise to be present every day until the consummation of the age, with all who gather his harvest in his name.

One final observation: Jesus' farewell promise discloses a messianic vocation that covers three generations, not one or two. His own work fulfills a unique vocation from heaven to earth. When he now says *Go,* he confers on Simon Peter and the other brothers a share in the same assignment from the same heaven. And when he further commands them to baptize and to teach a third generation, he extends the same vocation even beyond that "to the end of the age." The promise to be with them covers that whole continuing cycle. When, in carrying out his commands, they are themselves forsaken, the One whom they had forsaken will be with them, completing their education in the thoughts and ways of his Father.

So it is that Matthew brings to a close his account of the education of Simon Peter and his fellow students. Until they had all fled on the night of his arrest and until Peter had denied knowing him at his trial, they had failed every examination that had been set by their teacher. Matthew and his readers, however, knew that at least some of these students had, after their teacher's death, been empowered to join him in the covenant of the cup. At the end Jesus had succeeded in fulfilling the promise he had given at the outset: "I will train you as fishermen to catch people."[5]

Questions for Reflection and Discussion

1. As you read 28:18–20, consider whether this text is like (1) a baptism service for infants, (2) a reception service for confirmands,

(3) an ordination service for parish pastors or priests, (4) a commissioning service for foreign missionaries, or (5) none of the above? Discuss the problem of finding a similar use.

2. Have you ever thought of your own baptism as the conferring and the accepting of an authority from the living Lord? Would such a thought change your attitude toward your daily life?

3. "...teaching them to obey everything that I have commanded you": Are you among those here commanded to teach or among those taught to obey? In either case, Matthew seems to have you in mind in these passages: 5:3–7:27; 10:5–42; 13:3–53; 18:1–35; 23:1–25:46. Take time to read these again. A group concluding its study should set aside a special time for this reading, with each member taking reponsibility for reading aloud a section of the text. That reading might be followed by joining in the prayer of 6:9–13.

SUPPLEMENT 1

FISSION OR FUSION?

In examining this manuscript before sending it to the publisher, I have become aware of how foreign it will seem to many potential readers. This will be especially true for those who have been consulting the report of the Jesus Seminar or studies of Jesus that have been produced by members of that Seminar. From start to finish, my reading of Matthew has been grounded in his fusion of three perspectives (see pp. 2–4). From first to last the work of the Seminar has been grounded in the efforts to achieve the fission of those perspectives, tearing the few authentic teachings of Jesus loose from his concerns for training the apostles and from God's design in the gospel. The contrast will perhaps be clarified if I quote my correspondence in 1979 with Robert W. Funk, the chairman of the Seminar.

31 January, 1979
Dear Paul:

This is an invitation to join what the editors of *Semeia* and its advisors think is a most promising and exciting project. We are proposing to form A NATIONAL SEMINAR ON THE ORIGINAL SAYINGS OF JESUS. The seminar will endeavor to determine whether there is a scholarly consensus regarding what Jesus really said, and, if so, what that consensus is.

I am enclosing a copy of the description I prepared for the *Semeia* board. The description was adopted in principle by the board, but the specific terms of the seminar will no doubt be modified before we proceed...

After you have read the description, please feel free to raise questions with me regarding the proposal, either in its substance or in its format. I will not be able to answer all your questions until I have been able to meet with other members of the Steering Committee to iron out the rules...

We would like to learn from you whether you are interested in joining the seminar as a working member. Your commitment at this time need be only an expression of interest. As quickly as we know whether funding is available, we will ask you for a further decision. Meanwhile, we would like to proceed with planning on the basis of your tentative response.

Let me hear from you soon.

Most cordially,
Robert W. Funk

February 12, 1979
Dear Bob:

Your letter of January 31 is at hand with its invitation to join the seminar on the original sayings of Jesus. Thank you for the invitation and the detailed description of the project.

I must decline. I do so on conscientious grounds, compelled to do so by my conscience as both a historian and a Gospel exegete. To be fair to you, I feel impelled to outline the reasons why I must oppose the entire project. To the committee this opposition will probably seem to represent conservative theological scruples, but in my own mind it represents an effort to maintain scholarly integrity. I could not participate without violating principles that should govern my work as a historian and an exegete.

It is obvious that I cannot expect the organizing committee to understand these principles without further explication. It is also obvious that, to be adequate, that explication would require a book-length essay. That is impossible. I must be content with indicating as briefly as possible some of my major considerations...It will be an almost inevitable inference from what I say that I condemn those who have initiated the project. That is not my intention. Yet I must say that I can only view the project as decisive evidence of basic errors in historical methodology as applied to the Scriptures...In my remarks I have obeyed your injunction to "feel free to raise questions...regarding the proposal, either in its substance or its format..."

Yours sincerely,
Paul S. Minear

Some Reactions to the Proposal for a National Seminar on the Original Sayings of Jesus

The proposal claims for itself "intrinsic scholarly merit" or "genuine scholarly merit." I challenge such claims. It gives priority to "the relation of scientific biblical scholarship to American [*sic*] culture" but gives no consideration to the relation of that scholarship to the authors of the New Testament, to the church for which those authors wrote, or to the obligations of "scientific" scholarship to respect the character of the data with which it deals. In what follows I will try to indicate some basic considerations that lead me to oppose the project. These considerations may be summarized under six headings.

(1) The project presupposes untenable conceptions of what the Gospels are, of the original intentions of the Evangelists, and of how their writings should be interpreted. Therefore any success in the project could only demonstrate the scholars' forfeiture of their obligation to the sources and could only contribute to widespread popular misconceptions of the Gospels. The Gospels are narratives. In its forced separation of discourse from narrative, the project not only scorns the will of the authors whom scholars are pledged to respect, but it carries to a point of final absurdity the tendencies of two centuries in scholarship which Hans Frei has recorded and undermined in his *Eclipse of Biblical Narrative.* For example, the Evangelists were careful in most cases to relate Jesus' sayings to specific audiences (disciples, crowds, enemies, etc.). In its focus on the content of sayings apart from their narrative contexts, the proposal presupposes mistaken conceptions of the Evangelists' intentions in preserving any of the sayings. In the project's address to the general American public it would ignore the implications of the Evangelists' address to their immediate Christian constituencies. As I see it, then, the project can only produce wrong evaluations of those writers and writings whom we have pledged to "translate"– and I have indicated only a few of the points of "mistranslation."

(2) The project presupposes attitudes toward Jesus which as a scholar I cannot in good conscience endorse. It views him primarily as a teacher, whose vocation must be judged primarily by the general relevance and the wisdom embalmed in his words. His vocation as a *prophet* commissioned and sent to the Israel of his day cannot be adequately dealt with in a series of disconnected sayings. Moreover, the project tends to absolutize the fatal dichotomy between "the

Jesus of history" and "the Christ of faith"—a conceptualized abstraction that has bedeviled the history of modern hermeneutics. Whereas for the Evangelists and their readers, everything said by Jesus before the Passion derived new meanings, and often revised formulations, from their faith in the living Lord, this study would encourage the inference that all such changes would disqualify a "saying" from inclusion by the scholars. Thus the seminar should exclude from the beginning all scholars for whom *all* the sayings-traditions were preserved because of post-Passion faith and for whom the central thought of *all sayings* was affected by that faith (I think I would classify myself among or near this group). Certainly to vote for and to publish sayings which proved themselves immune to such re-interpretation would further confound endless confusions in regard to the relation between "the Christ of faith" and "the Jesus of history." Clearly all teachings dealing with such key matters as the kingdom of God and the messianic mission would have been affected by the life and worship of the early church; to eliminate them on the ground of such changes would guarantee a historically false picture of the situations both before and after the Passion. For me, personally, participation in the seminar would mean that I would be haunted by the ghost of Rudolf Bultmann and that of many other scholars whose insights regarding "the historical Jesus" would be tacitly rejected in a project like this.

(3) The project repudiates many of the chief hermeneutical advances of our own generation of scholars in various fields: literary critics, linguists, phenomenologists, structuralists, students of primitive myths, etc. It assumes that a series of disconnected sayings, chosen purely in terms of chronological and individual origin, can convey significant truths to a general audience. I think, for example, of these critics—M. Auerbach, *Mimesis;* Susan Sontag, *Against Interpretation;* Amos N. Wilder, *The Language of the Gospel, Theopoetic;* Paul Ricoeur, *Conflict of Interpretations;* S. Kierkegaard, *Training in Christianity.* Whereas the proponents of the project see it as marking an advance in methodology and professional expertise, I can only see it as marking retrogression in contemporary abilities to profit from recent advances in comprehension of the key literary forms. It will encourage diminishing respect for the imaginative components in the sayings tradition, for the aesthetic achievements of the Evangelists as "editors," and for the magnificence of the documentary results of their work (e.g., Can the Fourth Gospel emerge with anything but diminished status?). Can any results be anticipated that

would not be a modern expurgated *Diatessaron,* or, perhaps, more likely, a document resembling portions of the gospel of Thomas? Since it is impossible for us to agree on the contents of Q, can we really agree on the contents of a pre-Q–some imaginary collection that could have been formulated on the day preceding Jesus' arrest?

(4) The project not only embodies the triumph of an obsolete kind of historicism (I had thought that all sophisticated biblical scholars had jettisoned so obvious an exercise of "historicism"), it also assigns to a select group of historians an altogether obnoxious, if subtly hidden, brand of professional arrogance. "Who is able to do this?" "We are." It assumes a superiority of the present generation over their predecessors, as well as over the Evangelists and the early church. It represents the arbitrary appointment of a Supreme Court to determine by majority vote highly complicated matters of ancient history, and it assumes their freedom from any serious "conflicts of interest." Since, in terms of occupational situations, most of us as scholars are kin to the scribes of Jesus' day, this procedure gives to professional scribes an excessive authority in determining the cogency and relevance of the utterances of a prophet. It is really quite ridiculous for us, by accepting the goals and responsibilities outlined in the proposal, to assume the judicial robes assigned to us. How self-important can we get? How much do we really trust our "collective judgments" when we know full well the shaky bases of our own individual judgments? As I see our task in the modern world, this is *not* an important phase of that task. To accept it would be to acquiesce in major occupational pride and dishonesty. We have *not* been appointed to serve as a Supreme Court in this trial in which a wide range of innocent literary culprits will be quietly judged and found guilty.

(5) I am amused by the way in which "no-fault insurance" is offered to the potential jurors by the rules of the game. We are assured of full if not fulsome publicity for the results of our work and yet at the same time we are guaranteed full protection of our privacy in voting. We get the benefits of election to this high court, yet are protected from any "embarrassment." Most significant of all, we need not present, whether to any colleague or to any public, our individual or collective criteria or methodology. That provision effectively excludes from consideration the most decisive features! The criteria for our judgments are more important than the judgments themselves. To record the vote on a given saying but not the criteria that led to the vote is itself a basic methodological error that perverts

the whole procedure. It almost guarantees that we will as scholars be responding to the current scholarly Zeitgeist, that we will be engaging in uncriticized anachronistic distortions of the ancient texts, rather than allowing the texts to help us transcend that Zeitgeist and to avoid those anachronisms. We are to be freed from all the potential risks of voting, so long as we share in the anachronistic exercise of voting (no abstentions are to be permitted!). I must say that I have rarely seen so legalistic a procedure proposed for a group of qualified scholars. I assume that such fixed rules are necessary for the desired results to be assured—itself a sad commentary on the whole project.

(6) I could attempt to outline a final point, but I now realize that its explication would require longer than the *Semeia* committee is ready to read. Briefly, I believe the project is based on wrong presuppositions concerning the nature of *history* as lived, the nature of *history* as written, and the nature of the resulting work of historians, whether they are professionals who serve academic institutions or non-professionals who often have a sounder appraisal of both history and historians. The project is verbally and philosophically grounded in a question that American culture is now supposedly asking of scientific biblical scholarship—"What did Jesus really say?" Perhaps I have said enough to challenge this whole picture. I do not share this picture of American culture, this picture of scientific scholarship, or this formulation of the question. I believe that this question has been formulated primarily by a tiny segment of biblical scholars out of a laudable but misguided desire to make a fancied contribution to American culture, a contribution which in their own minds might justify their own existence. If I am wrong in these judgments (and in some degree I am bound to be), I pray for forgiveness. But I have felt an inner compulsion to express these criticisms, unmodified by qualifications which further direct discussions would, I am sure, make necessary. But I do ask you to weigh these remarks with some seriousness.

***

I have described my reactions in 1979 to the prospectus of the work of the Jesus Seminar. The first result of the Seminar's "Search for the Authentic Words of Jesus" has now been published: Robert W. Funk, *The Five Gospels* (New York: Macmillan, 1993). Two widely read bibliographical studies have also been produced by members of the Seminar, particularly Marcus Borg's *Meeting Jesus Again for the First Time* (San Francisco: HarperCollins, 1994) and John Dominic Crossan's *Jesus, a Revolutionary Biography* (San Francisco: Harper, 1994). A trenchant critique of these three volumes is now available in Luke Timothy Johnson's *The Real Jesus* (San Francisco: HarperCollins, 1996). Readers will notice substantial agreement between my prospective analysis written in 1979 and Johnson's retrospective appraisal.

What may now be said about the differences in perspective between the fission efforts of the Jesus Seminar and my efforts to do justice to the fusion of perspectives in the gospel of Matthew? I need to say something because readers may suppose that my study provides unintended support to the assumptions on which the Seminar's work was based. Have I not conceded that the Gospel, like all historical writing, told the story in retrospect from a later period? I have not even tried to separate the teachings or life of Jesus from the urgent needs and faith of the postresurrection church. In fact, I have insisted that in the narrator's mind all stories of the preceding period were fused with the training of the apostles and with faith in God's designs from the foundation of the world. For some readers such fusion can only distort all reporting on what happened before the crucifixion. Must we not be skeptical of such subjective views of objective reality, and especially dubious about all unsupported claims to guidance of earthly events by heavenly powers?

This is no place to deal in detail with so complex an issue. Even so, I want to point out some of the constructive results of the fusion of perspectives in Matthew. Every reader should be willing to give him and his faith a fair hearing. To that end I make a few bald assertions, trusting that the preceding chapters may furnish supporting evidence.

For Matthew as narrator, the retrospect of faith in Jesus as God's Messiah vastly enhanced the importance of what had happened earlier. It thereby enhanced his personal obligation to tell what had happened as it happened. Only this can explain the care with which he collected, organized, relayed, and interpreted those traditions about Jesus and his interns that had become accessible to him.

On the one hand, it would have been a personal betrayal of Jesus had he narrated the story without recognizing the divine designs embodied in it. Had he ignored the clarification of the story provided by its outcome, he would have rejected the key to its understanding and, in effect, would have left standing the verdicts of Caiaphas and Pilate.

On the other hand, his faith in that clarification placed the narrator under severe constraints not to distort the earthly contexts within which the kingdom of the heavens had come near. For example, his faith required that he show how the exaltation of the Messiah presupposed his complete humiliation as embodied in his work from the baptism to the execution. In this respect, faith in this Messiah required the rejection of dominant expectations of messianic power. Matthew's story must show such rejection. And it did.

The character of this messiahship also placed the narrator under the constraint to preserve the full rigor of Jesus' demands on his prophets-in-training to "be perfect as your heavenly Father is perfect" (5:48, alt.). The story must not minimize either the difficulties of repentance or the immediate accessibility of divine forgiveness. There must be no easy exemptions, excuses, or efforts at self-justification. And there were none.

The character of this Messiah's mission constrained the narrator to show how the assignment from the Father was such as to make fully intelligible the opposition on the part of Jesus' adversaries, who measured messiahship by human possibilities rather than by divine actualities, calculating power by Satan's scale rather than by God's. Such constraint is obvious; and it must be weighed against the fact that it magnified the narrator's own dangers from the same adversaries.

So, too, faith in the crucified Messiah constrained the narrator to give honest pictures of the blindness of the prophets-to-be in failing to see the signs of the kingdom. We have charted the difficulties the Messiah faced in the education of Peter and his colleagues and the ease with which they succumbed to Satan's views of messianic glory. Veneration for the apostles did not induce the narrator to weaken the contrasts between the little faith of Peter and the great faith of a Roman centurion and a Canaanite woman.

Scholars have rightly been alerted to the universal inclination in the writing and use of "history" to voice their own subconscious will-to-power and their own subtle drive for superior wisdom. Such inclination is always the enemy of truth. Study of Matthew persuades me that his faith in Jesus immunized him against that inclination to a remarkable degree. Jesus' induction sermon had made it clear to him that sheep become wolves when they rely on their own deeds of power (7:15, 22) or when they use their own piety to enhance public standing (6:1–18).

We conclude that Matthew's fusion of perspectives may have diminished one kind of objectivity, but it produced another kind: freedom from self-assertion, self-deception, and pride in standing before God. His story helped his readers discern the invisible roots and fruits of their own desires and actions, whether in God's kingdom or in Satan's. Modern readers should also treasure that kind of objectivity as a way of honoring the vast differences between their thoughts and ways and God's.

SUPPLEMENT 2

SCATTERED STORIES OR A SINGLE VISION?[1]

Among the greatest of the world's paintings is the gigantic fresco Michelangelo created on the wall behind the altar in the Sistine Chapel. I want first to comment on that mural. Having no competency as an art critic, I will rely on observations made by Roberto Salvini.[2] He stresses the fact that the painter rejected any use of a frame for his fresco. A frame would have implied "a fixed distance with a fixed viewpoint" (130–131). It would have presupposed a limited space and time whereas the painting was designed to cover the range of reality from the highest reach of heaven to the deepest zone of hell. The subject was too big for the room, for any room, for it pictured heaven with its dense population of angels and demons as the essential eternal context for everything that happens on earth, from the creation of the first mortal to the end of the age.

In the fresco, the focus of vision falls on the vindicated and powerful Judge. Near him on one side is a vast company of the patriarchs and prophets of the old covenant and, on the other, an equally vast company of apostles, martyrs and saints. At the bottom, on the one side, are the blessed who are being raised from their graves and, on the other, the cursed being assigned to Hades. Among the latter is "the extremely bitter self-portrait that the artist included in Saint Bartholomew's empty skin" (120). Essential to an understanding of the drama are the two lunettes at the top, one showing the Cross and the other the pillar, two symbols borne by angels to suggest qualifications that enabled the crucified Jesus to serve God as the final judge.

Let me make two additional comments. The fresco enables viewers to see synchronically the long story of earth within the context of God's creative activity. It also enables them to locate a single center for that story in the person of a human Jesus whose humiliation and exaltation embodied the power of God, thus qualifying him to serve as the judge of all. Because of the conjunction of these two, simultaneity and centrality, every episode in the long story points toward that center, which, in turn, yields an ultimate significance to each episode. The very scope and depth of this bond between detail and center justifies the location of the fresco behind an altar, where it invites the worshipers to see, once again, both the story in its unimaginable diversity and the center in its inexplicable synthesis of defeat and victory.

These comments introduce an explanation of the initiation and purpose of this essay, dealing as it does with selected incidents in the Gospel of Matthew. Let me state that purpose in various ways. Just as worshipers in the Sistine Chapel are being silently urged to hear again the witness of the patriarchs, apostles, and martyrs when they see the men and women in the fresco, so, too, readers of the Gospel stories are being subtly urged to relate each scene in the Gospel to the central scene—the crucifixion. To put the same point more technically: As Michelangelo provides a synchronic vision of a long tradition that happened diachronically, so Matthew edits a diachronic collection of stories in a way that calls for a synchronic vision. My purpose is to help readers view Matthew's Gospel as a single mural with a central scene, the scene of a helpless Servant whose very humiliation fulfills the divine hidden design in each of the preceding episodes.

But to see the Gospel in these terms is far from easy because of the emergence of modern attitudes toward history, the development of historical sciences, and the subjection of every verse in the Gospel to tests employed in those sciences. Those tests give priority at every point to the demands of diachronic reasoning. Every past event must be located at a specific point on a fixed chronology, after other events with their possible influences and before other events with their possibly warped interpretations. A chain of successive events must therefore be reconstructed before hypothetical influences and meanings can be ventured. Whenever Matthew relayed events out of their original order, any interpretation becomes more hazardous. Only a strictly diachronic reconstruction can lend credibility to the causes and effects within the story. And such causes and effects are limited to things observable in time and space. References to interventions by angels or demons arouse either outright disbelief or nervous skepticism. Even more embarrassing are appeals to heavenly kingdoms, whether divine or satanic, or to warfare between those kingdoms. Faith in a God from whom, to whom and through whom are all things, yet a God whose closest link to human history is by way of human hearts–such faith can only complicate historical narratives and their understanding. Yet that very faith is essential both to Michelangelo's Last Judgment and to Matthew's Gospel.

In spite of such difficulties, I want to challenge my readers to *see* the Gospel in ways analogous to Michelangelo's vision. And there is no inherent difficulty in meeting that challenge. In writing his Gospel, Matthew was himself seeing all its contents in retrospect. Like all memories, retrospects are by nature synchronic. All such retrospects receive their unity from being viewed by a single set of eyes that interprets earlier events in terms of present significance, whether destructive or constructive. This holds true also for Matthew's first readers or listeners. They were believers who had accepted from Jesus, as their Lord and Savior, an exalted and dangerous vocation. That vocation established as pivot in all their thinking the image of God's crucified Servant, a pivot that provided them with the key to grasping significances concealed within all the stories and teachings, the key of Jesus' own mission, viewed synchronically. Interpreters who fail to recognize the integrity of this retrospect, or who, in recognizing it, infer that it automatically invalidates their vision, will never see the stories as Matthew and his first readers saw them.

What was true for that original conversation of writer and readers is also true for some Christians today. They often listen to these stories during times of worship, introspection, and inward imagination. At the same time they are facing an altar on which a Cross continues to provide for that imagination the detailed recollection of the Passion–a recollection that is synchronic in the fullest sense. These worshipers are at times prompted by the presence of the Cross to see the connections between two moments: the moment of the Gospel lesson as read from the pulpit and the moment of that terrible crucifixion. Such a vision may well remind these worshipers that the church has placed the entire Gospel of Matthew in its canon of authoritative scripture, preferring the entire Gospel to any distillation of the earlier events that might seem more credible.

Now let me illustrate Matthew's synchronic perspectives by examining three episodes, selected from Chapters 11 and 12. These three are typical of many. They all focus upon sayings of Jesus that often fail to attract much attention from modern teachers and preachers; but I believe that inferences drawn from them carry important weight. Viewed diachronically, these sayings have proved very baffling to historical exegetes; but viewed synchronically, with the Passion story as the center, they give a clear and coherent witness to the good news.

1. The Blessing and the Offense

Now when Jesus had finished instructing his twelve disciples, he went on from there to teach and proclaim his message in their cities. When John heard in prison what the Messiah was doing, he sent word by his disciples and said to him, "Are you the one who is to come, or are we to wait for another?" Jesus answered them, "Go and tell John what you hear and see: the blind receive their sight, the lame walk, the lepers are cleansed, the deaf hear, the dead are raised, and the poor have good news brought to them. And blessed is anyone who takes no offense at me" (11:1–6).

In interpreting this story historians find many difficulties. The story-teller shows virtually no interest in the original participants. Apart from the reference to John and Jesus, there is no concern for those actors. None is named. No response to Jesus' answer is given. There is no clear location in space or time. No concern is shown for John, his reason for raising the query and his response to Jesus' answer. Six groups are mentioned as having profited from Jesus' work, but none of them is present and none speaks. Jesus gives no direct answer to the question, but instead leaves to others the responsibility for answering. In fact, he places the emphasis not on his own identity but on the judgment of others about him. He calls attention to the six groups who have responded to his message, though they are not even present. Only a few things seem to be common to the six: acceptance of the good news, through a repentance stimulated by their helplessness. Nothing is said about their political status. The only economic factor recognized is poverty, though the kind of poverty is unspecified. All six groups appear to be disadvantaged religiously, being subject to certain sanctions as unclean and thus disqualified from a full share in the worship of synagogue and temple. None is in a position of power, or in a position, when healed, to exercise power. In short, the characters in this story and their place in society are as undefined as the crowds in *The Last Judgment.*

Little wonder that an exegete finds it difficult to establish a context within which the story can be interpreted. Such a context is partially provided by "what you hear and see," but the very next statement of Jesus proves that this context alone does not fully answer the question. Nevertheless, the text does contain clues to that answer. Those clues are found in the saying of Jesus that forms a natural climax. What is the offense? Who are offended? Who are not offended? What is their blessedness? The Gospel as a whole provides clear and convincing answers to these four questions. We will answer those questions in order. When those answers are in hand we will know how to view this scene in its relation to the rest of the mural.

"No offense at *me*"...Jesus is himself the offense. It is not the signs that offend, but the person. Not his power to release captives, but his failure to present the evidence that would fit the expectations of "the one who is to come." He appeared rather as "a glutton and drunkard, a friend of tax-collectors and sinners" (11:19). He was too meek and humble in heart to qualify (11:29). He did not "wrangle or cry aloud," did not step on a bruised reed or extinguish a flickering lamp (12:19–20). An ordinary man, member of an ordinary workman's family, who received no special respect in his home town (13:55–57). Last of all and slave of all, he was of all penitents the most humble in heart (11:30).[3] All these offenses were telescoped into one: "I must go to Jerusalem and undergo great suffering at the hands of the elders and chief priests and scribes." That offense was too much even for his closest follower (16:21–23). Jesus not only lacked the expected credentials, he rejected them. His offense was to reverse all human measures of greatness, of freedom, of wisdom. When God struck down this shepherd, all the sheep in his flock scattered. He thus fulfilled his repeated warning: "All of you will be offended in me." All definitions of the offense meet in and are reflected from the forsakenness at Golgotha: Jesus *is* the offense. (That present tense remains a present tense through all generations.) He does not claim messianic greatness. Far from it. He epitomizes messianic lowliness.

Who are those offended? The Gospel mentions diverse groups. One is the generation of children who, playing in the marketplace, reject the calls from John as well as Jesus (11:16–19; 21:28–32). Another, the residents of Chorazin, Bethsaida, and Capernaum who refuse to repent, thus sharing in God's judgment on Tyre, Sidon and Sodom (11:20–24). Blindness to the presence of God's grace unites in a single obtuse generation those proud people from different places and times. The offended include "the wise and intelligent" whose self-esteem prevents them from seeing things revealed to infants (11:25). One must include Pharisees who, blinded by their own place on Moses' seat, could not accept the priority God placed on mercy (12:1–14). The key to all these offenses was something internal in the offended themselves, a self-assurance that inhibited complete honesty before God. They could not repent because of blind eyes, deaf ears, and hearts that could not understand the possibilities that opened up on the far side of complete humility before God (13:1–5). Nowhere is this definition of offense more inclusive and more devastating than when the Passover blood was being "poured out for many for the forgiveness of sins" (26:28).

Who are not offended? Obviously the fresco calls us to look in the opposite direction. One detail in the painting identifies the six groups who are specified in response to John's question (11:5). Another detail–the weary and overburdened who respond to Jesus' promise of rest (11:29). Another is provided by those who, bedeviled by demons, are freed from their blindness and inability to speak (12:22). Others, because of their abundant and understanding hearts, receive healthy eyes and ears (13:15–16). The parable of the seeds adds to our list those who hear the sown word, who understand it, and who yield God's intended harvest (13:24). Finally we must include those members of Jesus' school of prophets who, after being offended and scattered at his arrest, are humbled enough to accept his final assignment on the mountain in Galilee.

As Matthew paints the picture, this scene permits only two options: to be offended or not. There is no third possibility. Such a perspective permits only two results: to be blessed or cursed. The only ultimate source of blessing and curse is both invisible and inaudible: the eternally creating God. It is to his approval that Jesus refers in his declaration: "*Blessed* is anyone who takes no offence at me." In what, then, does this gift of blessedness consist? One inclusive answer is this: inheritance in the kingdom of God and rescue from the power of the Evil One (6:13). But there are many cognate metaphors for expressing such inheritance and rescue: the vision of God, the gift of an ultimate mercy, comfort for sorrow, life as children of God in the family of his Servant-Son, the healing of infirmities, freedom from fear, the strength and wisdom of the Holy Spirit, treasures in heaven for those who store them there, courage to save life by losing it, and, finally, the promise "I am with you always." This detail in the vast mural is painted in such a way as to point to its luminous center and to be illuminated from that center. The painter invited all his readers to share his synchronic vision of that reciprocal reality.

2. Before and After the Violence

As they went away, Jesus began to speak to the crowds about John:

What did you go out into the wilderness to look at? A reed shaken by the wind? What then did you go out to see? Someone dressed in soft robes? Look, those who wear soft robes are in royal palaces. What then did you go out to see? A prophet? Yes, I tell you, and more than a prophet. This is the one about whom it is written, 'See, I am sending my messenger ahead of you, who will prepare your way before you.' Truly I tell you, among those born of women no one has arisen greater than John the Baptist; yet the least in the kingdom of heaven is greater than he. From the days of John the Baptist until now, the kingdom of heaven has suffered violence, and the violent take it by force. For all the prophets and the law prophesied until John came; and if you are willing to accept it, he is Elijah who is to come. Let anyone with ears listen! (11:7–15)

This entire paragraph consists of an address given by Jesus to the crowds, who had gone into the wilderness to see a prophet whom Jesus now declares to be "much more than a prophet." In fact, no one born of women is greater than John the Baptist. He is the promised Elijah, whose coming is a fulfillment of the law and the prophets.

Here Jesus separates three periods: first, the period "until John came." Second, "from the days of John the Baptist until now." Third, the kingdom of the heavens, where "the least" are greater than John. In contrasting the first and third periods, Jesus clearly was posing a riddle: how can *the least* be *greater* than a prophet who is *greatest* among those "born of women"?

The riddle serves to focus readers' attention (Matthew shows no interest in the crowds' reaction) on the three periods, with special attention to the second: "since the days of John," a period during which "the kingdom of the heavens has suffered violence and the violent take it by force." Let us examine those three periods.

"Until John came…" This period explicitly embraces all those born of women, i.e., since Eve. It is a period when the law and the prophets constituted a time of prophecy (23:35–36). In the prophecy of John, that period had reached its term, for he was none other than Elijah, sent ahead of Jesus as God's messenger (11:10). That errand established John as "more than a prophet." All this, of course, was intelligible only to those willing to accept it.

"From the days of John until now…" This is the second period, with its beginning clearly identified. The text places Jesus as standing within this period, along with his audience (with Matthew and his audience as well). This second period, this *now,* describes the kingdom of the heavens as under attack from violent forces. That attack seems to have been initiated by John's announcement of the kingdom, by his baptism of those with penitent hearts, and by his identification of the "brood of vipers" (the progeny of Eve's serpent?). An early clue to the violence had been the struggle of Jesus in the wilderness with Satan, a struggle that had been provoked, in turn, by his penitence at John's warning. An early instance of violence had been John's imprisonment, mentioned in this very passage (soon to be followed by John's murder). The same brood of vipers charged John with being under the control of demons (11:18), rejecting any claim that his work had been authorized from heaven (21:25).

The rest of the Gospel so fully documents the human violence against Jesus as the spokesman for God's kingdom that its mounting intensity need not be reviewed here. In simple truth and with abundant proof, this prophet came to earth in order to bring a sword (10:34). In fact, this early period in his ministry led to a single result: his adversaries conspired how to destroy him (12:14). That goal clearly demonstrated the measure of the violence being unleashed, not only against him but also against his school of prophets (10:24–33). Such is one definition of the *now.*

So much for the violence that was aroused on earth when the good news was announced. Behind and within that war, Matthew discerned the outbreak of violence in the heavens between the two invisible kingdoms, one of God, the other of Satan. This conflict had been going on "since the foundation of the world" (10:34). The *now* marked the time when both John and Jesus disclose the advent on earth of God's victorious kingdom. In that disclosure was the assurance that God had cast Satan out of heaven so that his kingdom could no longer stand (12:25–29). Through this invisible victory of God, Satan's house had been entered. Its owner had been tied up and his possessions plundered. Of that plundering in heaven, Jesus' exorcism of demons provided the visible earthly evidence. True, the demons that were evicted from their house could return to wreak even greater damage. Such a prospect only called for greater alertness on the part of those who had been healed (12:22–23). Even so, the power of the Spirit of God had been so clearly demonstrated that to deny such power eliminated the further possibility of forgiveness. This terrible prospect seems to have been promised those who accepted the Word but who, on being persecuted for their faith in that Word, recanted their faith (13:21). These parables disclose the invisible bond between the heavenly and the earthly violence, each being "the flip side" of the other. The violence in the heavens is inseparable from the violence in the heart, caused by its divided loyalties. The victory over the primeval enemy in the heavens brings victory near the hearts that come under attack on earth.

"The least in the kingdom is greater than he…" This is the third stage in the sequence. We should not read this declaration as if it canceled Jesus' tribute to John. During the government by the law and the prophets, no one could be greater than Elijah. John's greatness was in his being a witness to the unprecedented opportunity now open to all those born of women. Their banishment from Eden had been ended in the mercies of God's kingdom, inasmuch as the powers of the serpent had been overcome. The good tree in the good earth again produces good fruit (12:33). Something greater than Jonah or Solomon is here (12:41–42). Eyes can now see what the prophets had long hoped to see (13:16–17). In fact, the descent of God's kingdom from heaven to earth has made it within the reach of a simple petition by the community of disciples, and, with that descent, their rescue from "the Evil One" (6:9–12). His gift of that kingdom constituted God's blessing on those who were not offended at Jesus. It was that gift that defined the greatness of the least. It is the severity of the violence that attended the advent of the kingdom that is the greatness of these "least." They are greater than the greatest in the pre-Elijah age, than all those born of women.[4] They have been freed from the kingdom of the Evil One by the power of the Holy Spirit (12:28). It is that power that enables the blind to see, the deaf to hear, the lame to walk. It has cleansed the lepers and raised the dead; it has expelled demons and fed captives. Sown on the good earth, the seeds of the good news have produced its abundant harvest. As children of God, they shine like the sun in the kingdom of their Father (13:38–43). All this is true, even though they continue to face attacks from the enemy, ample justification for the recurrent warning "Let anyone with ears listen!"

3. Something Is Here That Is Greater Than….

The narrator next paints two scenes that reflect the same radical shift from one realm to another. In the first realm the law and the prophets have reached their term. In the other, things concealed from the wise and intelligent are made visible to infants (11:26–30). Conflict emerges at the point of transition. Here is the first scene in its entirety:

> At that time Jesus went through the grainfields on the sabbath; his disciples were hungry, and they began to pluck heads of grain and to eat. When the Pharisees saw it, they said to him, "Look, your disciples are doing what is not lawful to do on the sabbath." He said to them, "Have you not read what David did when he and his companions were hungry? He entered the house of God and ate the bread of the Presence, which it was not lawful for him or his companions to eat, but only for the priests. Or have you not read in the law that on the sabbath the priests in the temple break the sabbath and yet are guiltless? I tell you, something greater than the temple is here. But if you had known what this means, 'I desire mercy and not sacrifice,' you would not have condemned the guiltless. For the Son of Man is lord of the Sabbath." (12:1–8)

It is difficult for a historian to make much out of this scene. Although it reads like a story, more than 80 percent of the words are words of Jesus. Many questions a historian needs to raise are not answered: What happened? To whom? When? Where? What caused it? What are the results? The text provides only the details that are needed to clarify Jesus' words, but no clue is given as to their impact on anyone. The narrator assumes that his listeners will understand Jesus' reply better than the original actors did. It is not so much a story as a scene from a larger tapestry. What the actors see depends on their residence. The Pharisees as residents of one realm see only the infractions of the law that they are responsible for correcting. To them the scene documents the guilt of the disciples and requires condemnation by the judges. But in Jesus' response, the government of the other realm appears. He declares the disciples innocent and their accusers guilty, a guilt that stems from not knowing what had taken place. They do not recognize in Jesus and his disciples the authentic successors of David and his companions. *Something greater than* David is here. Nor do they recognize them as authentic successors of the priests in the temple, who are exempt from Sabbath regulations. *Something greater than* the priesthood is here. More decisive still ("I tell you…"), *something greater than* the temple is here (Rev. 21:22).[5] To mark the shift from one realm to another, Jesus repeats what God himself had said through Hosea (6:6): "I desire mercy and not sacrifice." *Something greater than* the need for sacrificial offerings *is* here. (Note the present tenses. This emphatic phrase recurs again in 12:41, 43, with regard to Jonah and Solomon.)

The second snapshot of the two realms shows the depth of the conflict that marks the boundary between them (12:9–14). The conflict between the Pharisees and Jesus over the observance of the Sabbath resumes. The attack on Jesus is the same; his counter-attack is different. Having done what they condemn as a violation of God's command, he responds by appealing to their own behavior: "If one of you has only one sheep and it falls into a pit on the Sabbath, won't you grab it and lift it out?" At first this counter-attack seems to employ ordinary logic. Concealed in it, however, is something less ordinary. Involved is a more important law: An act of mercy is always lawful, as the previous incident shows. An additional consideration comes into play in the seemingly obvious remark: a man is more valuable than a sheep. This contrast reminds the listeners that one of the most familiar images of God is that of the Great Shepherd who cherishes and cares for his people as a flock of sheep (9:36, 10:6). Matthew's listeners would also recall the parable of the shepherd who leaves 99 sheep at risk on the mountain, in order to search for one that is lost (18:14). If Pharisees rescue a sheep on the Sabbath, how much more would God rescue a man! "How much more valuable!"…"I desire mercy…" By these hints Jesus judges his judges.

Perhaps Matthew had also in mind a less immediate nuance. The Sabbath was not only the occasion for Moses' commandment. It was also the culmination of creation, a day that God had blessed and hallowed. And the coming celebration of a Great Sabbath would represent the redemption of that creation in the gift of rest (11:29). All this, of course, lay beyond the horizon of the Pharisees. Not only had Jesus broken the law; he had defended such violations as a mark of the fulfillment of God's design for Israel. They began to plot his destruction, thus making very clear the kind of violence that is the gateway between the two "ages." The behavior of the Pharisees illustrates the time before; that of Jesus and his disciples, the time after; the conspiracy shows the incompatibility of the two.

Each of the three incidents we have examined finds its climax in words of Jesus. There follows a climax of all three, given entirely in the words of the narrator himself (12:17–21). First of all, he stresses the fact that the plot to destroy Jesus did not dissuade him from continuing his work of mercy. Many crowds followed him…"and he cured them all"! Such defiance of the scribes' challenge virtually guaranteed the success of the conspiracy. Moreover, Jesus continued the practice of encouraging–in fact, commanding–those who were healed not to advertise their cures. He did not want to be hailed as "the one who is to come"–at least, not yet. Such self-assertiveness did not comport well with his role as servant. His first answer remained in effect: "Blessed is anyone who takes no offence at me."

The narrator then affirms that this all happened in fulfillment of Isaiah's prophecy, in his eyes clear evidence that Jesus had not come to destroy the law and the prophets (5:17). This fulfillment proved that Jesus was a better interpreter of the scripture than were his enemies. Moreover, Matthew underscores the fact that *something more than Isaiah* is present, in that it is God himself now speaking through Isaiah–all the more reason for the long citation, and for stressing the relevance of every line in it. "Here is my servant!" That is to say, "These acts of mercy are acts not of my servant alone but of me, since he is only following my orders."[6] As indications of God's will, those acts indicate his design for all creation. Behind Jesus' freedom from self-assertion and self-advancement is this role of servant; undue publicity would belie such a role. Through the servant's very humility (11:29–30) God speaks his own final judgement (*krisis*) and the final victory (*nike*). The hope of the nations is vested in the authority ("the name") of this servant, acting as the judge and victor. Such is Matthew's confession, the witness of Isaiah, and the manifesto of God–a fitting conclusion to the three incidents.

Again I urge my readers to visualize the Gospel as a vast fresco with the crucifixion at its center, and with every scene pointing toward it and defined by it. To use a phrase from a well-known hymn: The Gospel "is the heaven-drawn picture of Christ, the living Word."[7] The assertion that this picture is heaven-drawn is not simply the idea of the hymn-writer; it is what God says through Isaiah and through Matthew. But first of all it is the picture-in-words of the works-of-mercy done by the servant. Earlier on, I commented on one major contrast between Michelangelo and Matthew; saying that the former paints a picture that focused on Jesus as Judge, while the Gospel picture centers on Jesus as the crucified. I am now corrected by this very text. Matthew here portrays the crucified servant as being both Judge and Victor (12:20).

SUPPLEMENT 3

GETTING FROM HERE TO THERE, OR FROM THERE TO HERE?

For more than six decades I have been absorbed in studying and teaching the New Testament. During that time there have been many changes, some superficial and some profound, in methods of study and in resulting patterns of interpretation. The most subtle and most profound of the changes has been the increasing abyss between the thought-world of biblical writers and that of their modern readers. As a result, the difficulties in penetrating the ancient perspectives have steadily increased. And each genuine success in such penetration increases the difficulty of sharing the discovery with modern readers. Thus, successful interpreters encounter the difficulty twice. They experience a double culture shock, not unlike that of Chicagoans who go to live for thirty years in Ulan Bator and then return to live in Chicago. The shock may, of course, be minimal if during their residence in Mongolia they never lose their footing in their homeland; otherwise, however, the strain can become almost unbearable. The latter situation is created when interpreters listen, really listen, to the New Testament text and when they allow that text to introduce them into the thought-world where that text is wholly indigenous. Never is that text fully indigenous to our world, for it could never have emerged in that world. To wholly understand it, therefore, requires genuine assimilation into the world that produced it. Serious listening to any text accepts that requirement. It is that built-in demand that produces the double culture shock. In this essay we illustrate this situation by focusing attention on three familiar texts, selected from the Sermon on the Mount.

The Matthean Horizons: The Kingdom of the Heavens

The address in the Lord's Prayer provides an essential clue to the thought-world in which the prayer is at home. In that world, the

Our Father displaces all earthly fathers, just as the family of those who know him as Father displaces all earthly families. The family's claim on this Father, and his claim on them, become, through the very act of praying, a mutual bond that bridges the distance between the Father's "location" in the heavens and the family's "location" on the earth.

The first three petitions, in turn, visualize the desired movement from the heavens to the earth, a movement in which the family's desires become responsive to the Father's desires. In its petitions, the family recognizes the full and unabridged priority of the heavens. Just as God's name is hallowed in the heavens, just as God's kingdom has come in the heavens, and just as God's will has been realized in the heavens, so now let these be done also on earth. What God has now done in the heavens opens up the possibility of a transfer to the earth of God's presence and power. The actual transfer of such power, however, remains subject to the convergence of the Father's design in heaven and the praying of his family on earth. The kingdom constitutes, as it were, the present homeland of this Father and the desired homeland of this family. What else, then, can be said of this homeland?

To think of this kingdom is to think first of this God. If one must think of place and time, the place and time of this kingdom is where this God rules and where this God's will is done. God is present, to be sure, throughout creation, but God's kingdom is the object of prayer only on the part of those whom God has chosen to make God's own.

In Matthew's vocabulary, the term *heaven* usually appears in the plural: It is the kingdom in the *heavens*. This suggests horizons so wide that they cannot easily be mapped. Why the insistence on using the plural? We may hazard a few guesses. Because mortals have many gods, each of whom must be granted a realm in which to be worshiped (e.g., Mammon). Because different tribes and nations cherish their own patron deities, each with its own glory and power. Because cities, too, have heavenly as well as earthly boundaries (e.g., Jerusalem). Because individuals have angels that represent them in the heavenly courts. Because the internet of heavenly-earthly communications calls for an unlimited number of angels. Because the heavenly wars bring into the field armies of heavenly soldiers. It is this diverse population of principalities and powers, gods many and lords many, angels and archangels performing many duties, that makes it impossible either to limit the number of heavens or to map their extent.

Matthew also found it necessary to speak of more than one kingdom of (or in) the heavens because there must be space there for both the kingdom of God and the kingdom of God's chief adversary, Satan. Both lords have had their servants on the earth since the outbreak of division in Eden itself. All human desires and fears, loves and hates, have their invisible roots and fruits in one of these two heavenly kingdoms. That explains why it is impossible to measure their shifting boundaries. Satan's kingdom is to be found wherever God's kingdom is being resisted. Whenever God becomes active in the heavens, Satan responds by subtle and devious counteractions. Both actions and counteractions have immediate repercussions on earth, within the minds and hearts of mortals. The final petition in the Lord's Prayer, for instance, implies that only the heavenly Father can rescue his family from the evil one, that is, from being ruled by this false father.

In his early chapters, Matthew announces that a decisive event has taken place in the heavens, where God has won the battle with Satan, evicting this primeval enemy from the heavens to the earth, where God is engaged in extending God's victory to the earth. In one acute analogy, Satan is compared to a strong person who has just been defeated by someone stronger, by a thief who has broken into the person's house and plundered the person's possessions. Such a victory, of course, can be discerned only by the alert eyes and ears of prophets, who recognize the heavenly victory that makes this earthly plundering possible. It is, in fact, that victory that prompted the message of both John the Baptist and Jesus: The kingdom of the heavens has now arrived at the doors.

That declaration evokes an inescapable double demand: Repent and believe this news. Belief requires eyes that can see signs of the kingdom's presence, by no means obvious. Repentance requires ears humbled by God's offer of the kingdom through an unaccredited, or even discredited, prophet, a humility that relies wholly on the reality of this kingdom. Such requirements are so extreme as to make entrance into the kingdom like passing through the eye of a needle. So extreme, indeed, that prophets are needed whose eyes and ears can detect signs that have long been hidden.

When called by the Father, each prophet needs, in turn, to enlist the help of others and to train them in this difficult vocation. So

John with his school of prophets is followed by Jesus with his school, each prophet training his interns to discern signs of the kingdom's nearness and to call others to enter the narrow gate. These prophets, with those students, at once provoke attacks from Satan and Satan's earthly cohorts. Of these attacks, Jesus' struggle in the wilderness (supported by his Father, the Spirit, and the angels) provides an initial paradigm, while his struggle in the garden provides a final epitome of the relative power on earth of the two heavenly kings. So much by way of sketching the map of that universe within which Matthew reports on Jesus' opening lecture to his school of prophets.[1] We now turn to the task of locating on that map three of the demands he made of those intern-prophets.

The Source of Truth

This was said to the ancient people of God:
    Do not break your promises,
    but fulfill every oath you make to the Lord.
But I command you,
    Do not use an oath of any sort—
    not by heaven, for it is God's throne,
    not by earth, for it is God's footstool,
    not by Jerusalem, for it is God's city,
    not by the hairs of your head, for only God
    can make one hair black or white.
Your *yes* must be *yes;* your *no* must be *no;*
    for Satan is the source of anything more than this.
                    (5:33–38, author's free trans.)

The interpretation of these commands requires careful consideration of their context. To whom did Jesus issue them? To his school of prophets. On what does the chief accent fall? On the prohibition of any and all use of oaths to support their words. The four examples are intended to cover all uses of oaths. Even more surely, the accent falls on his limitation of their speech to two simple words, because Satan is the source of anything more. By implication, when they use those words without the support of oaths, God will be both their source and their guarantor. So whenever these intern-prophets speak, their speech will come from one of those two heavenly rivals. Because so much is at stake in their simplest words, we must examine this strange demand to detect any nuance that may clarify the original rationale.

Earlier in this lecture Matthew has indicated that these prophets-to-be would be persecuted like the prophets before them. Already he has identified their probable persecutors: those who charge Jesus and his followers with violation of the laws of Moses (in this case Lev. 19:12; Num. 30:2; Deut. 23:21). This is the fourth instance in which Jesus demands of his interns a righteousness exceeding that of their adversaries (5:20). Whereas the scribes require the fulfillment of all oaths, these prophets must avoid even making such oaths. In speech as well as in forgiving their enemies, they must be as perfect as their Father. In his continuing battle with Satan, then, Jesus uses as a weapon the standard of absolute truthfulness, the same standard that rules the heavens. Because all speech comes from their hearts, it is a test of the purity of those hearts. This excludes the desire in speech to say something more or less than yes or no.

The seriousness of this choice of the heart becomes clear in the account of the situations they will face in their first fieldwork assignment. Then persecution will become more than a possible challenge. On his account they will be dragged before governors and kings (10:18). They will be forced to declare their loyalty to him, a yes or a no. The danger of death will tempt them to equivocate and to use more or less impressive oaths to prove their innocence. Would they then "have no fear" (10:26–39)? Would their fearless yes accept the loss of their lives for his sake?

Later, in fact, Matthew gives a transparent account of a prophet's speech that relied on oaths and that came simultaneously from a prophet's heart and from the evil one. On the occasion of Jesus' trial, his leading disciple was accused of association with him. In response, Peter swore profusely in his effort to support his frantic denials. In that same courtroom, in Jesus' yes God defeated Satan, and in Peter's no Satan defeated God. Only then did the rooster remind Peter of Jesus' earlier warnings. Such is the situation that gave a terrifying immediacy and finality to Jesus' prohibition of oaths and his demand for simple, though costly, honesty.

God's truth; Satan's lies; a human voice utters both. The words erupt from deep in the human heart, but the hidden origin of both voice and heart is one of the warring kingdoms in the heavens. For this reason, no human court is competent to judge in this area. The validation of all such speech belongs only in a heavenly court. Elsewhere Jesus says that mortals must give account in a heavenly court for every idle word (12:36). In this world, no human conversation can be limited to two persons; a third is always present. This is especially true in the world of Jesus' spokesmen, whose yes and no must reflect their origin in God's continuing struggle with Satan.

The Source of Security

Jesus' training of his spokesmen gives a central importance to three decrees that at first seem to be quite independent but on closer inspection reinforce a single demand. The appearance of independence stems from the choice of three separate images, those of treasures, eyes, and slaves. Their interdependence lies in their use by Matthew to disclose alternate choices made by the heart. In using these images, Matthew is concerned not so much with general ethical ideals as with the preparation of fishermen (Peter, Andrew, James, John, and others) to fish for people. That fishing will test their mastery of these instructions. First of all, their success will depend on their choice of investments. This free translation may identify the two options:

1. You must not store your treasures on earth.
2. There moth and rust devour them,
3. there thieves break in and steal them.
4. You must store your treasures in heaven.
5. There moth and rust cannot touch them,
6. there thieves cannot break in and steal.
7. Your heart will be where your treasures are.

(6:19–21, au. trans.)

The rhetorical structure adds force to the demand of line 4. The parallel structure of lines 2 and 3 declares that there can be no security for treasures stored on earth. By contrast, the parallelism of lines 5 and 6 declares the absolute security of treasures stored in heaven. The antithesis between lines 2–3 and lines 5–6 makes inescapable the prohibition of line 1 and the command of line 4. It is the fieldwork described in chapter 10 that also makes a choice between lines 1 and 4 inescapable. These prophets-to-be must store their treasures with the God who has called them and given them their assignment. Only with God is their investment secure. Neither the erosions of time nor the depredations of thieves touch the treasures stored with

God. For them there is no third option: earth or heaven. At this point, the thought embodied in lines 1 through 6 seems to be complete.

Line 7, however, is a carefully chosen climax that shifts the thought away from the careful calculation of self-interest. Jesus' concern is not with the safe investment of money but with the location of the heart of his workers. Heaven is the only place where their heart is secure. Only hearts that store all treasures in heaven can make authentic the announcement that the kingdom of the heavens is at the door, along with the demand for repentance and complete trust in that kingdom. By their own act of treasuring, Jesus' interns can demonstrate the truth that, since heaven is where their heart is, their heart is where heaven is. God's heaven and human hearts belong together.[2]

1. The body's lamp is the eye.
2. When your eye is single,
3. your whole body is full of light.
4. When your eye is evil,
5. your whole body is full of darkness.
6. So, if the light *in you* is dark,
7. everything is dark!
(6:22–23, au. trans.)

Because of its importance, the eye has become in all countries a favorite metaphor that carries many different cargoes. Among biblical uses, two are combined in this rather opaque analogy. Because blindness keeps light from entering the body, the eye is a lamp illuminating the whole body (line 1). Because it is through the eye that an object outside the body arouses desire (e.g., 5:29), a single or undivided eye represents a strong passion within the body for that object. If that passion is evil (line 4), the whole body is shut off from the light, and darkness is total (line 5). By underscoring the importance of the eye, this metaphor thus underscores the greater importance of the desire: Is it single and undivided, or divided and therefore evil?

The link to the previous demand should be clear. The evil eye is deceived by the evil one and therefore desires treasure both on earth and in heaven. The single eye desires treasure only in heaven; so, too, the link to the following law: The evil eye is slave to two masters, the single eye, to one. When we remember the field assignments of these intern-prophets, we immediately see the direct force of this analogy. As they face hunger and hostility, uncertainties and hurdles that seem impossibly high, will their eye be single, storing all their treasures where their heart is, or will their eye be evil, deceived by the evil one into thinking that they can serve two masters? The work will disclose their choice, the light or the darkness. "You are the light of the world."

> It is impossible for you to be a slave of two masters.
>   You will either hate the one and love the other,
>   or you will be devoted to one and despise the other.
>   You cannot be a slave both to God and to Mammon.
>   (6:24, au. trans.)

This declaration clearly reflects a slave economy where everyone recognizes the complete authority of masters and the complete subservience of slaves. Here Jesus uses that economy as the basis for an analogy of the human relationship to God. In *this* heavenly economy, every powerful human desire and loyalty registers the power of some invisible lord. For every lord, there are slaves on earth; for every slave, a lord in the heavens. It is impossible for anyone not to be a slave of some lord. Because of the multiplicity of human desires, it is almost the universal fashion to be a slave to many lords. This is so obvious that many interpreters have concluded that contrary to Jesus' law, it is impossible to be the slave of only one lord. We all have too many competing loyalties for that.

In this case, however, Jesus was issuing a rule for an audience limited to those committed to work in his harvest field and to love his Father alone. That vocation demanded that they hate and despise any other master, such as Mammon. For them the impossibility has become a necessity implicit in their work. This impossible possibility was a measure of the impossible possibility of God's kingdom. Their work of announcing God's reign made their possessions, their Mammon, an attractive alternative. But to be a slave to their Master they must abandon those possessions. Without purse or suitcase, they must beg for food and lodging in hostile towns. In fact, their message would increase that hostility. Other folks might hide their divided loyalties behind various subterfuges and easily deceive themselves; not so these slaves.

Matthew provides clear examples of the two options. When Jesus summoned a hated tax collector to follow him, his positive response was immediate. He began his service as a host to Jesus, his students, other tax collectors and sinners. Shortly thereafter, when Jesus sent those students on their risk-filled mission, this man accepted with the others the assignment as a slave of one master (9:9–13; 10:3, 5–39). Jesus invited another man to sell his possessions and to join the others in the same work, but this man went away "grieving." He, too, demonstrated the truth that a rich person cannot enter the kingdom of the heavens. Only those willing to become last of all and slave of all meet the standard (19:16–26). To modern readers it may be more intelligible to substitute the image of soldiers instead of slaves. For soldiers in an army that is engaged in battle, it is impossible to obey generals on the opposing sides. To obey one is to hate and despise the other. For Jesus and his school, these opposing generals commanded their forces from heaven; the victories of God in heaven now made possible victories on earth, but such victories could be won only by soldiers with a single treasure, a single yes, a single commander.

The Source of Daily Food

We turn now to examine the specific petitions in what is commonly called the Lord's Prayer. Originally, of course, it was not designed for Jesus but for students in his school whom he was training for their later work. To bring out some of the latent implications of this prayer, we translate it freely.

> Our Father in the heavens:
> Just as you have extended your authority over the heavens,
>   so now extend your authority over the earth.
> Just as you have established your kingdom in the heavens,
>   so now establish it on the earth.
> Just as you have carried out your plan for the heavens,
>   so now let it be carried out on the earth.
> (6:9–10, author's trans.)

As we have observed, the address clarifies many dimensions in that world that the prayer itself helps to create. The term *Father* identifies not only the deity being addressed but also those who are praying as his family. The pronoun *our* implies their character not as an association of individuals but as a community bonded by mutual affection, dependence, trust. In very specific ways this Father has spoken to this family; the prayer epitomizes their response. This speech and response is a point of convergence between the heavens and the earth, the invisible and the visible, the authority, power, and design of the creator and the response of his creation. This family has accepted the prophet's revelation: "The kingdom of the heavens is at the doors"; it has believed, repented, and rejoiced in the Father's mercy. The word from above has evoked this response from below; now the call from below begs the Father's response from above. This line of communication between Father and family creates bonds stronger than those among other human families (10:35–37).

This new creation is evidence that, as the first three petitions say, the Father's name is at last hallowed throughout the heavens, his power to rule there has been vindicated, his plan has been realized there. God's victory over Satan in the heavens has now become accessible to his praying family. The prayer expresses the desire for that victory. The subsequent petitions indicate four battle zones where need for the Father's help is most acute.

> Today, provide us with manna sufficient for the day
> > (as we carry your assignment on earth)
> Today, forgive us our sins against you,
> > as we forgive our enemies' sins against us.
> > > > > (6:11–12, au. trans.)

The fourth petition voices needs that these intern-prophets will experience in their work. Jesus forbids them to take along with them any food and any money to buy food. They will depend on the prospect of handouts from homes along the way. The provision of bread by their hosts will represent, from day to day, God's answer to this petition. Each meal will represent a heavenly gift through earthly caregivers.

Soon after he dictated this petition, Jesus provided a shocking analogy to that situation. In their fieldwork, they will be like birds that do not store their food for the next day but rely on each day's search. Just as their Father feeds the birds, he will also feed them. But should they, like sparrows, starve to death, that, too, would be in accord with their Father's will (10:29–33). However, worry is forbidden. Any anxiety would indicate a lack of faith in their Father (6:28, 30–33). Only complete trust in him will qualify them to announce his kingdom to all the hungry.

The story of Jesus himself provides a timely illustration. His own prophetic call had been followed at once by a struggle with Satan in which a forty-day fast had opened the way for a major trial of his reliance on his Father. Jesus did not become anxious but had learned from scripture how to deal with hunger. He remembered the story of Israel's forty-year wandering in the wilderness. During that long trial, God had humbled God's people "by letting you hunger, then by feeding you with manna…in order to make you understand that one does not live by bread alone, but by every word that comes from the mouth of the LORD" (Deut. 8:1–3). This manna, this food from heaven, could not be used on the second day. Similarly, in their fieldwork, Jesus' messengers would be dependent each day on food from heaven, like Israel in the wilderness and like Jesus during his first trial.[3]

There is a further relevance to Matthew's account of Jesus' sustenance by God's word in the wilderness. We have seen how the first three petitions were based on the conviction that God has already won a victory in the heavens over Satan and that this victory now makes possible victories on earth. If we ask *how* such a victory had been won in heaven, one cogent answer is this: Jesus' victory over Satan in the wilderness. There is impressive evidence to support that answer. Victory came only after God had declared Jesus to be God's beloved Son and only after the Holy Spirit had descended on him. That same Spirit led Jesus into the wilderness, where no one was present but God's Son and Satan (not Satan's earthly servants but their master). Only in the heavens could Satan transport Jesus to the roof of the temple. Only from the heavens could all the kingdoms of the world be seen in one glance and offered as a bribe. Only there could angels minister to Jesus. It was there that Jesus' victory was won by God and the Spirit of God, a messianic event indeed. Simultaneously, of course, the victory was won on earth by a very human Jesus, vindicating his own baptism of repentance. It could thus become a pattern for his disciples in their work on earth. In that work, this anxiety-free petition for daily manna became a point of entry for Jesus' power over Satan on earth and God's power over Satan in the heavens.

The fifth petition, like the rest of the prayer, derives its meaning from its context in the story as a whole. In that story the Passover provided the prime example of God's forgiveness. In the passover sacrifice, God struck down the shepherd of God's flock. In the passover meal, that shepherd poured out his blood "for many for the forgiveness of sins." In that supper and that sacrifice, the word *sins* was defined both by the hatred of Jesus' enemies and by the betrayals by his own disciples. So the daily prayer of those disciples, by their forgiveness of their enemies, extended the range of God's mercies. God's love for good and evil, Jesus' forgiveness of his enemies, the disciples' extension of that forgiveness—all illustrated the transfer station where God's will was being done on earth. At the very point where the weak forgave the strong, the power of God was perfected in human weakness. For disciples to refuse to forgive would be to betray this power. In using this prayer, the disciples confessed that there was only one answer to the question, How many times to forgive? Yet no reader of this Gospel should underestimate their desperate need for this fifth petition.

> Do not bring us into the time of trial,
> but rescue us from Satan's kingdom. (6:13, au. trans.)

"The time of trial" is no vague reference to some petty infraction of a moral injunction. Jesus destroys such an illusion. A single comparison underlies all of his instructions: like teacher, like students. No student can be above his teacher. None can claim immunity to the same tasks or the same hazards. Like the teacher, the students must carry the cross. It is the prospect of the cross that defines "the time of trial." Nothing more clearly defines that time than the story of Gethsemane. It is there that Jesus used what can accurately be called the *Lord's Prayer*. "Sit here while *I pray...My Father...*" The account leaves no doubt as to the intensity of struggle—"even to death." Matthew seems to indicate that Jesus suffered more anguish in Gethsemane than on the cross. Throughout his mortal combat, Jesus recognized that the outcome depended wholly on his Father's will. "*If it is possible,* let this cup pass from me" (26:39). (In the disciples' prayer a similar recognition is expressed in *"bring us not* into a time of trial," 6:13, au trans.) Implicit here is the possibility that God can exempt Jesus from drinking the cup. But the following words make several things entirely explicit: "Not what I want but what you want" (26:39). (This is equivalent to the disciples' "your will be done"). Thus, Jesus prays, in effect, "May your name be hallowed...may your will be done". By defining the time of trial, these words also define the rescue from Satan.

The Gethsemane story thus serves to interpret every petition in the prayer Jesus taught his disciples. It disclosed how they, too, could be rescued from the evil one. However, the story issues a blunt and terrible judgment on those very students. First, Jesus appeals to them to stay awake with him. Then he appeals three times in mortal agony to his Father. And three times he comes and finds them asleep (surely one ingredient in his agony). Each time he gives them a stinging rebuke. "Stay awake" (a warning that recalls many parables). "Pray that you may not come *into the time of trial*" (26:41, the same words as in their own prayer). Jesus' prayer in Gethsemane thus embodies two victories: God's victory over Satan in Jesus' trial and Satan's victory over God in the trial of the disciples. On Golgotha, a few hours later, both of these victories are demonstrated in the interlocked stories of Jesus and Peter. Golgotha and Gethsemane together give mysterious breadth and abysmal depth to all seven petitions in the disciples' prayer. In each petition, heaven touches earth and supplies the source, sustenance, and goal of their vocation.

***

We are now in a position to probe into the dilemma with which this study began. How may we best cope with the double culture shock that is experienced when we move from our modern thought-world into Jesus' thought-world and then from his world back into ours? The problem reminds me of the name of a street near the center of Bristol, England: "There and Back Street." That street is a cul-de-sac only a few yards long. One can easily walk there and back in a few seconds. How much longer the way back to the world of Jesus and Matthew! That street spans remote places and times, complex languages, and even more complex cultures. We can, of course, summon the help of many archaeologists, historians, linguists, and theologians to help us get there, but the journey is never easy or short, even with expert help.

Another difficulty, however, makes it almost impossible to get there from here. This difficulty confronts us when we note how Jesus' own contemporaries failed to comprehend the kingdom of God and the struggle with Satan. At his crucifixion, how many people understood his words or actions? To be sure, many were confident of doing so, but he could with truth say that no one recognized him as son of his Father, and no one recognized God as Father of this son (11:25–30). He lived and thought in a world that he was unable to share even with those whom he had been training for months, whom he hoped would have eyes and ears to see and hear what had long been hidden. If they could not fathom the mystery, how much more difficult for us? The story of Matthew itself provides the measure of the difficulties in getting there from here.

In Vermont there are many versions of the yarn about the farmer who, on being asked by a stranger for directions to a certain town, replied, "You can't get there from here." Our problem has a similar impossibility. In fact, many biblical scholars confess that this ancient thought-world is no longer accessible to "modern man." Some scholars declare that the message of the kingdom cannot even be translated into modern languages. In any case, efforts to get there are quite futile. I am inclined to agree. I want to point out, however, that what makes it impossible for scholars may be their own fixed residence and their satisfaction with their own thought-world.

It is abundantly clear that one cannot get to a full acceptance of Jesus' commands in the Sermon on the Mount without radical movement in his direction. We have seen where he located the source of truth, security, food, and forgiveness. We can understand those commands only by rejecting human efforts to locate such a source *here.* Access to his thought-world requires simultaneous rejection of Satan-inspired human views of both the *there* and the *here. There* he saw the victory of God's kingdom over the enemy kingdom; *here* he demanded penitence, trust, and a life of slavery to a new master. For him, an absolute priority belongs to God's movement from the *there* to the *here.* Many hymns remind us that it is from the highest heaven that he comes to us. First comes God's victory there, and then comes the revelation here of that victory. First comes the call to penitence and trust and then the human response to that call, faith emerging simultaneously with the sense of a new vocation that matches the heavenly vision. Thus, a new map of both the heavens and the earth becomes accessible to God's family on earth.[4] So when we listen intently to the Gospel, when we accept the good news of God's kingdom, when we join in the petitions of the Lord's Prayer, when we receive the Passover body and blood, the gift of grace becomes as amazing as the apostles declared it to be. The shock of receiving that grace is greater than any culture shock, ancient or modern.

NOTES

Chapter 1

[1]The remoteness of this horizon is due in part to Isaiah's distance from us and in part to his awareness of distance between all mortals and the Eternal. Paul Ricoeur is one interpreter acutely conscious of both distances: "The purpose of all hermeneutics is to conquer a remoteness...By overcoming this distance, by making himself contemporary with the text, the exegete can appropriate its meaning to himself: foreign, he makes it familiar, that is, he makes it his own...By understanding himself in and through the eyes of the sacred, man performs the most radical abandonment of himself that it is possible to imagine." *Conflict of Interpretations* (Evanston, Ill.: Northwestern University Press, 1974), pp. 16, 22.

[2]The term *imagination* is being increasingly used in many fields of scholarship. In literary criticism, Amos N. Wilder, *Imagining the Real* (St. Petersburg, Fla.: Possum Press, 1978); in sociological analysis, Benedict Anderson, *Imagined Communities* (London: Verso, 1983); in theology, Garrett Green, *Imagining God* (San Francisco: Harper and Row, 1989); in biblical exegesis, the works of Walter Brueggemann, who writes, "The biblical text, in all its odd disjunctions, is an offer of an alternate script, and preaching this text is the exploration of how the world is if it is imagined through this alternate script." *Theology Today* 52 (1995): 320.

[3]The centrality of Jesus in the narrative is shown by the fact that no episode takes place without reference to him and his mission. A possible exception is the account of the death of John the Baptist (14:1–12), but even that account begins and ends with Jesus. Another exception might be Judas' meeting with the chief priests, though again this is a fulfillment of Jesus' own prediction (26:3–5, 14–16). This concentration on Jesus' presence may explain why there is no account of the meeting between the women and the disciples, as ordered in 28:7–10.

[4]Throughout the Gospel the picture of these adversaries remains quite vague. Only group terms are used: scribes, Pharisees, priests, rulers of the synagogues. Until the high priest enters the scene in chapter 26, no adversary is named. They function only as a group. No issue is joined one-on-one. All issues are seen in black and white terms. All matters under debate are used to clarify Jesus' position. To serve this function, the adversaries do not even need to be present (23:13–37). As in the case of the crowds, no attempt is made to provide an objective profile of these groups. Whether explicitly or implicitly, their opposition is traced to the heavenly struggle between two opposing kingdoms.

[5]It is, of course, difficult to speak in any book today of "the ways of God." Susan Sontag has spotted the origin of that difficulty: "Of all possible crimes which an entire culture can commit, the one most difficult to bear, psychologically, is deicide. We live in a society whose entire way of life testifies to the thoroughness with which the deity has been dispatched," *Against Interpretation* (New York: Farrar, Straus & Giroux, 1966), 249.

[6]This sense of God's presence does not merely add another aspect to the perspective of Matthew; it pervades the whole: "Through imagination sanctified by God's Spirit, the saint sees everything as related to divine mystery...The saint sees the world stamped as part of God's creation and subject to God's intervening wrath and love." H. P. Simonson, *Andover Newton Theological School Quarterly* 16 (1975): 115.

[7]It is possible that many modern readers may sense their kinship with the disciples through their own vocations, which have come to them from "outside" themselves. "A rediscovery of the supernatural will be, above all, a regaining of openness in our perception of reality...It will be an overcoming of triviality. In openness to the signals of transcendence the true proportions of our experience are rediscovered." Peter Berger, *A Rumour of Angels* (New York: Penguin, 1970), 119.

[8]Among the exceptions, 12:49 may be mentioned; there the relation of the disciples to the crowds is not entirely clear. Another is 8:18–22, where two men who have not completely broken their ties to their homes may be spoken of as disciples, though that very requirement is the occasion for their mention. The clearest exception may be found in Joseph of Arimathea, who arranged for the burial of Jesus (27:57–60). We must look more closely at that incident.

Matthew clearly speaks of him as one who had been discipled to Jesus (the verb is used), even though he had not shared in the mission work of the Twelve (chap. 10). That he dared to ask Pilate for the body reflects at least some loyalty to Jesus. That Pilate was willing to grant his request reflects a degree of identity with Jesus' adversaries. In fact, both Mark and

Luke speak of Joseph's membership in the Sanhedrin, though Luke adds that he had taken no part in their verdict. Those evangelists did not call him a disciple; they spoke of him as one who was expecting the kingdom of God. John's was the only other gospel that called him a disciple, albeit one who kept such loyalty secret "through fear of the Jews." John made Joseph and Nicodemus (a member of the Sanhedrin) partners in anointing and burying the body.

So the story of Joseph is highly complex and uncertain, in part because of its strategic location. We conclude, however, that even though Matthew called Joseph a disciple, his readers would not classify him with the "school of prophets," but would be aware of a strong irony in such classification. For one thing, Matthew called him a rich man, after making wealth and discipleship quite incompatible (19:21–22). That detail linked the Gospel story to Isaiah's declaration: "They made his grave with the wicked and his tomb with the *rich*" (53:9, emphasis added).

Moreover, Matthew shaped his story in such a way as to link it to another text in Isaiah (22:16). Of all the accounts of Joseph, Matthew alone indicated that the tomb was one that Joseph had hewn out of the rock for himself. Those details coincide with Isaiah's report in which the steward Shebna was expelled from his office because he had cut out a tomb in the rock for himself. Those two texts in Isaiah not only have relevance to the Matthean text, they accent the presence of irony in identifying Joseph as a disciple. Similar irony may be seen in his kinship with the Twelve in their frantic betrayals, denials, and flight. Irony may also be detected in the contrast to what had already happened at the death of Jesus. The quake that had already ripped open the tombs of the saints rendered entirely useless a burial in a tomb hewn out of the rocks. Even more ironic, perhaps, is Joseph's futile effort to make the tomb secure by rolling a great stone over its door. Such an effort was as misguided and futile as the action of the adversaries in posting a watch over the tomb. Friends and enemies agreed at least in misunderstanding what had happened! From all this one is impelled to conclude that the reference to Joseph as a disciple may have been an intentional contradiction in terms that revealed more substantial truths.

[9]Much of chapter 23 appears to be a duel with his opponents, but this is more apparent than real. No mention is made of their entrance or exit, of how they provoked his attack, or of how they reacted. The seven woes were heard only by the disciples (or the readers), as disclosures of heaven's judgment and as warnings about their own behavior when they replaced the scribes now sitting on Moses' seat. Here Matthew (or Jesus) was using the adversaries as stock figures to illustrate the magnitude and insidiousness of the hypocrisies that are perennial threats to the future leaders of God's people.

[10]Matthew's concern for the training of these fishermen is one of many things that distinguish the Gospel from a biography of Jesus. A biography would have given much more attention to his home and early experiences. References to his father disappear after chapter 2. After Jesus left home, his mother and siblings are mentioned only twice, and one of them speaks of their replacement by a new family (12:46–50). From chapter 4, Jesus' sole concern is with his ministry to the crowds and his training of the disciples. So the story as a single unit is not the biography of an individual but of a group, a group bound together by a shared vocation from God.

[11]In beginning to study any book, readers have a right to know the particular angle from which the author approaches his topic. How does an author conceive of his own interest in what he writes? To answer that question in this case, let me say that I view my role as a critical biblical theologian in terms similar to those of Garrett Green, who writes: "The religious vision of 'what the world is like' embodied in the scriptures of the Old and New Testaments is for Christians the paradigmatic norm for human life and thought. Christian faith can be characterized accordingly as 'faithful imagination'–living in conformity to the vision rendered by the Word of God in the Bible. Theology is one function of the faithful life, performing the task of critical interpretation…A truly critical theology performs the task of interpreting the imaginative language of scripture on behalf of the community seeking to live in conformity to its vision." *Imagining God,* p. 134. Basic to this language-world is a distinctive sense of ultimate reality, an ontology that is vastly different from all one-world conceptions, whether ancient or modern. See also my essay, "Ontology and Ecclesiology in the Apocalypse," *New Testament Studies* 12 (1966): 92–93.

[12]In most settings, Matthew speaks of the heavens in the plural. He always writes "the kingdom of the heavens" and "my" or "your" Father in the heavens. God is imagined as speaking from the heavens. On occasion the singular is used, as, for example, when heaven is paired with earth, or when the reference is to things visible from earth like birds or clouds;

then the word *ouranos* should be translated *sky*. Why the plural elsewhere? *Heavens* allows more room for hierarchies of principalities and powers, for many rulers in the heavenly places. It gives room for the invisible but decisive conflict with the devil and the devil's angels, as well as for the armies of angels worshiping God or representing individuals or nations. The plural more readily encompasses the imagined beginning, renewal, and end of all things, the inclusion of all times and places, all generations and tribes. At the least, Matthew's plural preserves continuity with scripture where the plural appears much more frequently than the singular, for example, in the Psalms, Isaiah, and Jeremiah.

Chapter 2

[1]This chapter is based on an essay published in *Interpretation* 51 (1997): 31–41.

[2]Later stories indicate the difficulties in categorizing the "faith" of these crowds. The first parable of the seeds divides them into at least four groups, all accepting the seed but all subjected to the power of Satan's deceptions (13:1–9). They hold at least three different views of Jesus' identity (16:14). A more complete analysis of the crowds–disciples relationship appears in "Gospel Studies in Honor of Sherman E. Johnson," *Anglican Theological Review* (1974): 28–44.

[3]For a recent study of the roles of the disciples in Matthew, see David E. Orton, *The Understanding Scribe* (Sheffield: Academic Press, 1989), 153–68.

[4]In verse 11 the NRSV reads "when people revile you…" The term *people* is altogether wrong in representing the third person plural of the Greek verb. Reviling is never by "people" in general. We must understand this subject *they* by reference to other Matthean texts in which these opponents are identified.

[5]For a more thorough analysis of Matthew 10, see chapter 3, and also my *The Golgotha Earthquake* (Cleveland: Pilgrim Press, 1995), 110.

[6]Cf. *The Golgotha Earthquake,* 56–61.

[7]Among many New Testament passages in which the work of Jesus brought changes to the earth, I have selected these for special study:

John 8:2–11: Jesus writes twice on the earth. *Horizons in Biblical Theology* 13 (1991): 23–37.

Luke 2:8–20: The angels announce peace on earth to the shepherds. *Christians and the New Creation* (Louisville: Westminster John Knox Press, 1994), 1–30.

Matthew 5:5: Jesus pledges the earth to the meek. Ibid., 118–20.

Matthew 27:47ff.: God's shaking of the earth in the crucifixion. *Horizons in Biblical Theology* 17 (1995): 62–83.

[8]It is significant that when the gospels speak of the authority of the Messiah and his disciples to forgive sins *on earth,* this forgiveness changes the relation of the forgiven to the earth.

[9]There are major similarities between Matthew's perception of perfection and the perception in the epistle to the Hebrews. Compare, for example, Matthew 5:48 and Hebrews 12:23.

[10]Cf. *The Golgotha Earthquake,* 60–61.

[11]Cf. my essay "Far as the Curse Is Found," *Novum Testamentum* 33 (1991): 71–77.

[12]Cf. *The Golgotha Earthquake,* 101–6.

[13]In Matthew's thought-world, a mountain was the proper place for communication between the heavens and the earth. Here Satan's strongest lure was exerted (4:8) and God built the city on the mountain (5:14). Here the Messiah gave his disciples their initial and final lessons (5:1; 28:16). Here Jesus talked with the earlier prophets and God commanded the three apostles to obey God's Son (17:1, 9). When those apostles faced impossible odds, they were instructed to flee to a divinely provided refuge in the mountains (24:15–21). When Jesus needed to consult with God, he retreated to a mountain, distancing himself from the clamant demands of the crowds and enabling him to watch the distant boat in which his students were struggling with turbulent waves and winds. The night spent on the mountain gave him power to deal with their fears and faithlessness (14:23–33). The mountain where they failed, but he succeeded, in feeding the crowds—a lesson that they did not grasp—reminded readers of the setting for the Sermon on the Mount (15:29–38; 16:10–12). So, too, mountains provided the best locale for a parable that revealed and tested the prime qualification of a good shepherd. A human shepherd is pictured on a mountain, guarding a large flock. If he is a true shepherd, he will risk everything to find a sheep that has been led astray (the Greek verb suggests that it

has been deceived, either by a false teacher or by persecutors). The editor placed this parable in a chapter where apostles are held responsible for communal discipline. Their determination not to lose a single sheep must match "the will of your [God] in the heavens" not to lose a single one of "these little ones" (18:10–14).

[14]In these two tiny parables of the salt and the light, Matthew shows a tendency to combine diverse images to identify a single sacred space: the mountain, the city, the house, the place of instruction, and the presence of God. In this fusion of images, the narrator echoes Isaiah (Isa. 2:13; 4:5; 56:7).

Chapter 3

[1]The relevance of these parables becomes quite dramatic if they are read after Matthew 10 or after Matthew 28.

[2]Notice this direct allusion to the welcome accorded the centurion at Abraham's table, because many modern exegetes have stressed the contrast (and perhaps conflict) between Matthew's legalism and reliance on works and Paul's antilegalism and reliance on faith alone. Paul and Matthew did not agree on all points, but this reference to Abraham and the Gentile shows that the contrast has been greatly exaggerated.

[3]The novelist Reynolds Price tells of a vision, during his long struggle with cancer, in which he met Jesus alongside the Sea of Galilee. In this vision he received from Jesus a similar assurance of both forgiveness and healing. *A Whole New Life* (New York:Atheneum, 1994), 42.

[4]When Jesus invited those who carried heavy burdens (11:29), these were probably the same burdens, referred to in chapter 23, that the scribes refused to carry, thus locking the burdened out of the kingdom of the heavens. To this dramatist, this pride of the scribes and Jesus' humility were ultimate enemies.

[5]Cf. my essay, "A Theology of the Heart," in *Worship* 63 (1989): 246–54.

[6]The constant difficulties that Peter and his colleagues experienced in understanding and obeying the demands of Jesus add credibility to their portrait of his teaching and work, for followers do not often invent such difficulties for themselves. Why should they create a phantom who, in turn, creates such difficulties? Each successive difficulty adds to the weight of this evidence, which also helps to explain the mutation of some sheep into wolves, and explains, in turn, the Master's condemnation. It is little wonder that Peter, like the others, wondered if the rewards would prove to be adequate compensation for the sacrifices–additional evidence of the rigor of the Master's demands (19:27–30). Because some readers may not have a concordance at hand, let me give here all the Matthean references to Peter:

4:18	Jesus' call and the initial response
10:2	Naming as the first apostle
14:28–29	Peter's lack of faith in the storm at sea
15:15	Peter's failure to understand an important parable
16:16–18	Simon bar Jonah as Rock
16:22–23	Peter as Satan's mouthpiece
17:1–4	Misunderstanding a heavenly vision
17:25–26	Ignorance about the temple tax
18:21	Misunderstanding unlimited forgiveness
19:27	Uncertainty about the rewards for service
26:23–25	Unreadiness to die with Jesus
26:37–40	Asleep in Gethsemane
26:58–75	A threefold denial

Only in one case after Peter's appointment does Jesus appear to approve of Peter; in that case the approval is of God's revelation and not of Peter's insight or fidelity. The education of Simon Peter shows him moving from one error to the next, each becoming more serious and therefore less praiseworthy. The climax comes in the triple denial, which demonstrates his inadequacy for the mission entrusted to him.

Chapter 4

[1]As an essential tool for thinking about the unseen but real world, the term *heaven* seems to have lost its hold on contemporary language and thought. Poets, however, have not been so ready to discard the word as meaningless:

Heaven is so far of the mind
That were the mind dissolved,
The site of it by architect
Could not again be proved.

'Tis vast as our capacity,
As fair as our idea,
To him of adequate desire
No further 'tis than Here.

Emily Dickinson, *The Poems of Emily Dickinson* (Boston: Little, Brown & Co., 1930), 330.

[2]In his own way, Matthew would, I think, basically agree with this command from the original Methodist Covenant Service:

Get these three principles fixed in your mind–

That the things eternal are much more considerable than the things temporal;

That the things which are not seen are as certain as the things that are seen;

That upon your present choice depends your eternal lot.

Cf. Gordon Rupp, *Last Things First* (Philadelphia: Fortress Press, 1964), 2.

[3]Instead of being called birth stories, these stories should be called oracles of God's hidden purposes, which would be revealed in the following chapters. As oracles they give priority to the activity of heavenly forces: the Holy Spirit, dreams, angels, guidance by stars, fulfillment of prophecies. Their significance lies in such things as the following:

- the coming fulfillment of God's covenants with Abraham, David, and the prophets of the exile;
- similar fulfillment of promises made to Israel regarding the salvation of the Gentiles;
- the adoration of the heavenly king by Gentile kings and his rejection by Israel's king;
- a new exodus from Egypt;
- the identification of God's Son and Messiah;
- a father's acceptance of that Son in spite of the offense;
- the release of the Holy Spirit to guide all that follows.

[4]Matthew's description of the Pharisees as an evil and adulterous generation distinguishes his tradition from that of Mark (Mk. 8:12).

[5]Throughout the Pharisaic-messianic discussion, we may detect the conflict between two baselines from which thinking proceeds. From the baseline of earth, Jesus' proclamation of the kingdom and his demand for repentance could only be viewed as a double self-contradiction. The kingdom of the heavens could not be at hand because there were none of the expected signs: great changes in political, economic, or religious balances of power, changes that would be greeted with triumphal celebrations, public excitement, and the fulfillment of many earthbound hopes. The demand for repentance also involved intolerable contradictions: to demand total self-humiliation on the part of leaders who were committed to quite different standards of righteousness, standards that were expected to gain divine approval by God for those who had long served God and divine condemnation for those considered outcasts and sinners. So great was the offense produced by these two self-contradictions that Jesus pronounced all who were *not* offended by him to be God-blessed. That could be true only from a baseline view from heaven.

[6]In virtually every use of the term *bread* in this Gospel, readers should detect at least a double meaning: one when bread is viewed from the earth and the other when it is viewed from the kingdom of the heavens (4:3, 4; 6:11; 7:9; 15:33; 26:17, 26). These texts give priority in significance to the bread of heaven, although both types of bread are sources of sustenance for daily life.

Chapter 5

[1]The term for assembly appears only twice in Matthew and never in the other Gospels; it is therefore anachronistic to use the word *church* here. By contrast, the image of a house appears frequently (5:15; 10:6, 25; 12:25, 29; 15:24; 21:13; 23:38). That image appears in the use of the verb "to build" (*oikodomes*).

²It may be that poets are better qualified than historians or theologians to deal with the apparent anomalies in scripture. Theodore Spencer, for example, gives his reactions to the role of Peter in this passage:

> Jesus, wise in the knowledge of human weakness, looking in Peter's face,
> Forseeing the dawn's denial and the fear,
> Seeing in Peter's dog-like loving eyes all men's uncertain wobbling,
> Said to Peter, "You are the rock; *Tu es Petrus*," and smiled.
> "On a rock like you, like this, I build my church."
> The words are remembered too well; wise irony is forgotten.
> Forgotten the shake of the head and the sad forgiving smile.

(*An Act of Life* [Cambridge, Mass.: Harvard University Press, 1944], 70.)

³W. H. Auden has been able to catch in verse some aspects of the biblical views of Satan as "the great schismatic who/First split creation into two":

> Poor cheated Mephistopheles,
> Who think you're doing as you please
> In telling us by doing ill
> To prove that we possess free will,
> Yet do not will the will you do,
> For the Determined uses you,
> Creation's errand-boy creator,
> Diabolus egredietur
> Ante pedes eius–foe

("New Year Letter," in *The Collected Poetry of W. H. Auden* [New York:Random House, 1945], 277.)

⁴To recognize this "firm link," readers must read everything that happened in "the district of Caesarea Philippi" as a single story. Unfortunately, the NRSV breaks up this story into three sections with separate captions: Peter's declaration about Jesus (vv. 13–20); Jesus' foretelling his death and resurrection (vv. 21–23); the cross and self-denial (vv. 24–29). These captions destroy the tight logic embedded in the unbroken narrative, a logic that binds together four truths:

1. It is the death of the Messiah that qualifies him to give the keys to Peter, and it is his resurrection that invests that gift with God's own authority.
2. It is the cross-bearing of these interns that will qualify them to receive these keys from their teacher and will invest their apostolic work with God's authority.
3. The mutual self-denial and cross-bearing will assure their coming reunion with the Son of man, with his angels, and with his God in the glory of the kingdom.
4. The very keys that open the gate to that kingdom will lock that gate against those interns who set their mind "on human things" (16:23) by wanting to "gain the whole world" (16:26).

⁵No translation of this phrase can carry its original range of associations. The *Amen* frequently appears in a liturgical setting in a two-way conversation between the earth and the heavens. When spoken from the earth to the heavens, the *Amen* signifies hearty human approval of the doxologies and prayers addressed to the Divine. When spoken from the heavens to the earth, the *Amen* carries God's validation of the words spoken by God's human messenger. Accordingly, the Messiah is "the Amen, the faithful and true witness, the origin of God's creation" (Rev. 3:14). Or, as Paul wrote, "In him every one of God's promises is a 'Yes'" (2 Cor. 1:20).

Such is the language-world in which this phrase, "*Amen*, I tell you," belongs. In Matthew it appears more than thirty times. It is always spoken by Jesus and, with two exceptions, always spoken to his school of prophets at salient moments in their education. It carries an intangible and mysterious weight of reliability, authority, and finality. In most instances it expresses a stark warning or a firm promise. The series of warnings begins as early as their induction (5:20; 6:2, 5, 16). The promises are scattered widely (10:23; 13:17; 19:28). Both promise and threat are used to reveal the point of the final parable (25:40, 45). In all these *Amens*, Jesus speaks as arbiter of righteousness and as judge of his students' fidelity.

Chapter 6

[1]Jesus' attack on the scribes and Pharisees as the current shepherds and his promise of new shepherds for God's Israel are no less vitriolic and unconditional than Jeremiah's attack on the shepherds of his day (23:1–4). In fact, this evidence of continuity in prophetic generation and vocation may lie behind the popular identification of Jesus with Jeremiah (Mt. 16:14).

[2]There is a strange contradiction in Matthew's pictures of the crowds. On the one hand, their penitent trust in the advent of God's kingdom remains central to the plot, from their introduction in 4:24 to the end. On the other hand, the specific pictures of those who were healed remain vague and undeveloped. They are central to the divine commission of Jesus "to shepherd my people Israel" (2:6). Their immediate trust in the advent of God's kingdom makes them God-blessed as heirs of that kingdom (4:24; 5:3). By freeing them from captivity to Satan, God has revealed God's prior victory over Satan in the heavens (12:28). Their trust in God's assurance of that victory shows that, unlike the scribes and Pharisees, they have not been offended by the *kenosis* of this messenger (11:2–9, 25–30). Their presence in the story serves as an essential sign of the consummation of God's age-old design.

Yet, for all that, these signs remain strangely lifeless and voiceless. Not one of those healed is named. One after another they enter the stage without explanation and leave it without a trace. Not one plays any continuing role in the story. They find a common bond, not with earlier earthly associations, but only with their earlier status as lost sheep who have been shut out of Israel by their present shepherds, and who are now welcomed by Jesus and by new shepherds appointed by him (10:5–8; 23:34–38). Yet the camera does not stay focused on any case study of repentance. In fact, various parables of the sowing of seed reveal the dire uncertainties that separate harvest from planting (13:1–30; also 12:43–45). In short, the penitent lepers and demoniacs have an essential role, but it is that role and not their individual stories that alone explains their presence.

Why, then, this contradiction? Our investigation suggests a double answer. First, as we have argued from the beginning, in Matthew, Jesus' primary concern has been the training of the Twelve for their future roles as shepherds. That training received its climax in the celebration of Passover in the upper room and in Gethsemane. Second, when we look more closely at the final chapter, we discover a feature of Matthew that will be most surprising. Matthew designed his entire story to be read not by the believers (the sheep) in his churches, but by their shepherds. From first to last, he carries on a conversation with the "prophets, sages, and scribes" whom Jesus sends to replace the scribes and Pharisees who have forfeited their appointment to "Moses' seat" (23:34–38). From 5:20 on, Jesus has required of these newly appointed shepherds a righteousness that exceeds that of the defaulting shepherds. It is the chasm separating the true shepherds from the false ones that the entire Gospel clarifies. On such a clarification the destiny of the flock depends.

[3]In his story of Kierkegaard, George Steiner discovers the source of "miracle-working power" on the part first of Jesus and then of his apostles:

> The authenticating mark of the apostolic is an existential humility of the most radical kind. The true Apostle is humbled beyond all other humiliations known to man. Hence the rebellious terror, the surge of refusal, with which Old Testament prophets respond to the charge which God puts upon them. An Apostle is, at any given moment–be it in a street in Nineteenth century Copenhagen, or in a synchronic correspondence with the *humilitas* of Jesus, of the mocked, scourged, spat-upon and done-to-death Jesus of the Passion…Only the man or woman contemporaneous, "synchronzed with," that suffering Christ and compelled to speak, to exemplify the meaning of that suffering, can be held to reveal God…where it is fully analogous to that of Jesus, humility is total powerlessness, a finality of impotence…

("No Passion Spent," [New Haven, Conn.:Yale University Press, 1996], 262–63.)

Chapter 7

[1]The obtuseness of the apostles provides ample proof of the rigor of Jesus' demands. If those demands had been less difficult and dangerous, they could readily have demonstrated fuller understanding and obedience. Martyrdom is not often accepted as something required by faith in God.

²The story of Peter and the other disciples during this last week in Jesus' life offers a full documentation for several observations by Paul Ricoeur concerning the realistic conception of sin in the New Testament. "Sin inhabits man more than man commits sin." Sin is the power that binds humans and holds them captive. There is a communal dimension that indicates a metaphysical solidarity of the human race in sin. Sin constitutes a mode of being that is more radical than any individual act. (*Conflict of Interpretations*, 282f.)

³It is not hard to explain why this final pledge at the supper table has disappeared from eucharistic liturgies: It is almost impossible to update it. It contains its own protection against anachronistic revisions, since it tells of a nonrecurring time, place, personnel, situation, and prediction. There are other obvious reasons, as well, why this final moment in the conversation is easily forgotten; such a loss of memory, however, diminishes the original force of the covenant itself.

⁴For the subsequent role of this cock in literature, painting, and music, see George Steiner, *No Passion Spent* (New Haven, Conn.: Yale University Press, 1996), 370–77.

Chapter 8

¹This chapter is based on an essay that appeared in *Horizons in Biblical Theology* 17 (1995): 62–8.

²Donald Senior, *The Passion Narrative According to Matthew* (Louvain: Leuven University Press, 1975), 2.

³Ibid., 337.

⁴Cf. *The Golgotha Earthquake*, 84–94.

⁵This linkage between forsaking God and forsaking "yourselves" is an important clue to biblical thinking about the intimate bond between God's action and human action, both present in the heart's decision.

⁶The Greek verb "to cry" (*kradzo*) carried with it an ominous apocalyptic finality. This aura appears most clearly in Revelation. The souls of those slain cry out from under the altar (6:10). So the woman clothed with the sun cries out for the delivery of her male child (12:2). The angels cry out in announcing judgment on Babylon (18:2), as do the multitudes of the redeemed, chanting "Salvation...to our God" (7:10). In Matthew the verb also often belongs at the point where the authority of heaven collides with earthly powers. Confronted by the Messiah, the demons cry out (8:29). The blind men cry out to him for mercy (9:27). When disciples saw Jesus in the storm walking to them on the water, they cried out in fear (14:26). Such cries have the power to penetrate the barrier between the heavenly and the earthly, expressing deepest agonies and ultimate aspirations.

⁷Cf. my essay, "An Apocalyptic Adjective," *Novum Testamentum* 12 (1970): 218–22.

⁸In many of Rembrandt's paintings, reality is portrayed as a mysterious darkness within the light and a light within the darkness, both darkness and light being essential to the reality. So also in Matthew's description of the darkness at noon and daybreak at midafternoon. In both, the transcendent is not infinitely remote, but close at hand.

⁹Cf. Senior, 166–69.

¹⁰Christians have always been loath to admit the degree to which this earthquake shattered confidence in their own religious practices and institutions. We constantly need Jürgen Moltmann's reminder: "He who was crucified represents the fundamental and total crucifixion of all religion" (*The Crucified God*, 37). Only by the inclusion of Christianity within "all religion" can Matthew and his successors be freed from the charge of anti-Semitism.

¹¹Gordon Rupp speaks of the cross as "a mercy seat—a kind of Lidice, Buchenwald, Leningrad in reverse, in which revenge and hatred have been swallowed up in love and reconciliation." *Last Things First*, 34.

¹²Matthew's awareness of a radical contrast between the two Jerusalems can be easily overlooked, but it is integral to his thought-world. One Jerusalem is that holy city that is entered by the holy ones who are freed from their tombs by God's shaking of the earth (27:53). The other Jerusalem is the city that kills those same holy ones (23:37). See *New Testament Studies* 12 (1966): 97–100.

¹³Cf. *Golgotha Earthquake*, 48–51.

¹⁴The question whether anyone on earth heard the centurion's confession did not trouble the narrator. The absence of any notice by bystanders is as amazing as the confession itself. The Gospel is full of incidents when equally amazing things happened that escaped notice by

others. Had these things been visible or audible they would have created widespread publicity. Rather, they point to the thoughts and ways of God, which elude human measurement. The following is a partial list of such incidents:

The star the magi followed	2:9
The murder of Bethlehem children	2:16
John's words about Jesus	3:11–15
The heavenly voice at baptism	3:16–17
Healing a centurion's servant	8:13
Wilderness feeding of thousands	14:13–21; 15:32–39
Healing a Canaanite girl	15:28
Jesus' meeting with Moses and Elijah	17:19
Healing two blind men	20:29–34
Cursing the fig tree	21:18–22
Darkness at noon	27:45
Destruction of the temple curtain	27:51
Opening the tombs	27:52
A centurion's confession	27:54
The Easter earthquake	28:2

Chapter 9

[1]See Luther A. Weigle, ed., *The New Testament Octapla* (New York: Thomas Nelson, 1962), 182–83.

[2]We have seen how important in Matthew's world is the reality of the heavens. That fact renders his Gospel almost unintelligible in our thought-world. As Gordon Rupp has observed, "Hell vanished from our pulpits a hundred years ago, heaven fifty years later" (*Last Things First*, 62). It is impossible for those from whom heaven has vanished to make any sense of this entire interlocking story. At least it must be said that those who have been baptized in the triune name are homeless if heaven has vanished from their world.

[3]It may be observed that the disciples had already received this authority (10:1–6). That being true, this new authorization would seem, at least in Matthew's own perspective, entirely unnecessary; that is, unless we choose the second option.

[4]This way of viewing everything on earth from heaven "as a baseline" and of viewing these human sheep as divine shepherds may be construed as examples of the conception of theology advanced by Garrett Green in *Imagining God*, 138–42. I would add to Professor Green's analysis only this amendment to bring his worldview into line with Matthew's: The imagining should include not only God but also the heavens, the struggle between opposing kingdoms in heaven, the victory of God's kingdom over Satan's, and the release of God's power on earth to liberate those bound by Satan.

[5]If this interpretation of the final commission is valid, it follows that the entire Gospel was written with the needs of this specialized group in mind, the successors of that original contingent of "prophets, scribes, and wise [persons]." That would mean that among all the books of the New Testament, only Matthew sought to fulfill the needs of this limited group within the churches, the leaders, whom Matthew addressed under many metaphors: fishermen, shepherds, harvesters, slaves, apostles, teachers. In writing primarily for Christian leaders, then, Matthew had in mind the specific problems they would face in their efforts to make disciples; he did not probe all the problems that would be encountered by all Christians. On such problems other New Testament authors may be of greater help.

Supplement 2: Scattered Stories or a Single Vision

[1]This essay appeared under the title "Seeing the Good News" in *Theology Today* 55 (1998): 163–74.

[2]Roberto Salvini, *Michelangelo* (Milan: A. Montadori, 1976). Eng. Trans. A. Montadori, 1978. Subsequent page references are to this book.

[3]Jesus' indifference to messianic titles has gone unrecognized by later followers who have exaggerated the importance of such titles. This has encouraged a popular misunderstanding of the conclusion of his assignments in chapter 10 in which he distinguishes three groups of people who offer food and shelter to his apostles. Some welcome the apostles,

thinking they wielded authority or had come in the name of Jesus as "a prophet." Other hosts suppose the apostles wield the authority of Jesus as "a righteous man" (in Matthew's terms an important religious leader). Still others suppose that the apostles come only with the authority of "a disciple." For all three hosts, however, the commendation is the same: in welcoming his apostles all welcome Jesus and in welcoming Jesus all welcome God! It is their welcome and not their idea of his status that determines the outcome (10:40–42). This is true even if a host welcomed an apostle as one who carried *only* the authority of Jesus as a disciple of John the Baptist! Within Matthew's thought-world, the notion that Jesus might indeed be a disciple of John was by no means foreign. In 11:11, 13 Jesus gives a very high estimate of John's role in God's plan. In 14:2 Herod links the two prophets and, when John was beheaded, John's disciples reported his fate to Jesus (14:12), who then sought solitude for himself. When Jesus asked for popular perceptions of his own role, the first answer was "John the Baptist" (16:14). Finally, in his final trip to Jerusalem Jesus strongly implied that the two prophets exercised authority from the same source (21:23–32).

⁴This contrast between the greatest of those born of women and the least in the kingdom is similar to the contrast between those born of the will of man and those born of God in John 1:12–13. Also Matthew's identification of the coming of the kingdom with the reception of the Holy Spirit (12:28) is similar to John's identification of the vision of the kingdom with being born from above (3:3).

⁵Something greater than the temple: this is an almost explicit reference to the shaking of the earth at the death of Jesus with its destruction of the temple curtain (27:51). It also recalls the assurance of the collapse of the temple buildings (24:2).

⁶Matthew had no difficulty with the idea of a God who speaks. In that respect, many modern readers do have great difficulty. The most recent thorough effort to deal with this contrast is N. Wolterstorff, *Divine Discourse* (Cambridge: Cambridge University Press, 1995).

⁷William W. How, "O Word of God Incarnate" (1867), *Pilgrim Hymnal,* p. 252.

Supplement 3

¹A similar summary of Jesus' message concerning the kingdom may be found in M. E. Boring, *The Gospel of Matthew. New Interpreter's Bible* (Abingdon Press, 1996), viii, 288–93.

²Compare my essay "A Theology of the Heart," in *Worship* 63 (1989): 246–54.

³This association of bread with manna may explain the use in the Lord's Prayer of the very rare Greek word *epiousion,* usually translated "daily." Like the manna, the disciples' bread will be good only for one day.

⁴Before Matthew transcribed the texts we have studied, his personal imagination, as well as the imagination of his community, was very active. Within each petition of the Lord's Prayer, for instance, he visualized multiple intersections between the text and life. Each petition opened up potential "itineraries of meaning" that linked the *there* to the *here.* The action of reading the text and using the petition indicated an eagerness to follow those itineraries. Whenever that happens, the imaginations of Jesus, his interns, Matthew, and of generations of readers can become present in the imaginations of those who use the prayer next Sunday. For further analysis of this interplay of imaginations, see Paul Ricoeur, *Figuring the Sacred: Religion, Narrative and Imagination* (Minneapolis: Fortress Press, 1955), 144–49.

INDEX OF AUTHORS

INDEX OF PASSAGES IN MATTHEW